SMALL SPARKS OF LIFE

Published by

Librario Publishing Ltd
2005

ISBN: 1-904440-58-4
(First published 2001 by Gopher Publishers UK. ISBN No 0-9542960-5-2)

Copies can be ordered via the Internet
www.librario.com

or from:

Brough House, Milton Brodie, Kinloss
Moray IV36 2UA
Tel /Fax No 00 44 (0)1343 850 617

Printed and bound in Great Britain by
CPI Antony Rowe, Chippenham and Eastbourne

Small Sparks of Life

by

Lysanne Sizoo

Librario

To PER ANDERS
My Loyal and Steadfast Friend

Preface

A Swedish guy and a Dutch girl meet in a newsroom in London. The beginning of a fairytale, or so we thought. We married in 1990, at St. Martin-in-the-Fields, right in the very heart of London. The bright and happy ceremony the crowning glory on a life that had so far been chugging along smoothly. A year after the wedding, broodiness kicked in big time and I started to dream about us becoming parents. I kept imagining myself as a mother, and caught myself smiling knowingly at young mothers out pushing their prams. After much debate we finally decided that after the summer we would flush the pill down the loo and make sure to have a lot of fun trying. I was ready, enthusiastic and naive. Ready to embark on the next phase of my life. However, Mother Nature had other plans. For probably the first time in my life I was going to be confronted with serious failure. I might have been ready, but Life in her infinite wisdom was not. Having fallen pregnant within four months of trying, I lost my pregnancy at thirteen weeks.

In the period following my miscarriage I found myself in an emotional no-woman's land. Neither the career woman, nor the mother-to-be. I searched desperately to find someone or something to identify with, yet all I saw were pregnant girlfriends, pregnant cousins, and pregnant sisters-in-law. All successfully carrying their babies to term, without a hitch. It was painful and added insult to injury. After resisting the very notion that I was not coping and that I needed help in coming to terms with my loss I finally found and accepted help through a local miscarriage support group. It was being there that helped me to realise that there were other women out there who were experiencing similar feelings of loss, failure, and even hate. I learned that, however disturbing to me and my surroundings, my feelings were normal, and part and parcel of a grieving process. That sense of recognition was a great comfort.

No one who said "You're young, you'll have another one", or

"Miscarriage is quite common you know" knew how hurtful these well intended comments were. We didn't want another one, we wanted the pregnancies back that we had lost.

It has been many years now since the first of our miscarriages, but I can still remember the pain and bewilderment of those early days and the tremendous sense of failure that overshadowed everything else in my life at the time. Yet I've moved on, and I've found that there is of course life after a miscarriage. A good life too! We were blessed with a little boy, Karl, a wonderfully funny, happy little person, who managed to sneak into our lives just when we least expected him. I can truly say that I'm more than content with that one precious gift, now, but this book is about the struggle of the journey that got me to that point, about coming to terms with the fact that for us, 'having children', was never going to be easy. I hope that what I have written will give comfort to those who need it, and understanding to those who haven't themselves experienced the devastating effect of a miscarriage on a couple's life. It's not only about me, and about my feelings, it also very much about Per Anders (Peter), my partner, who suffered as much in the process as I did, though in a very different way. Our partners often have to bear the brunt of the anger and resentment that surfaces, and not only we, but also the outside world tends to forget that they too are suffering. At times they hardly have a chance to deal with their own feelings, since our feelings seem to outweigh them all.

Since that glorious day at St. Martin-in-the-Fields, through five miscarriages and the birth of our Karl, my loyal and steadfast partner has been there for me. This book is also a tribute to him, to his steadfastness, his loyalty, and to the fact that he turned out to be the best father in the world.

How lucky we are to have been able to find that out!

Small sparks

Small sparks of life
that burned so briefly.
Small sparks of life
I loved so fiercely.

Small sparks of life
never to be,
Small sparks of life
I set you free.

Small sparks of life,
never to have lived.
Yet small sparks of life,
you were a gift.

Chapter 1

THE FIRST SMALL SPARK

My period is late. I've never been this late. In fact, I've never been a day late in my life. So I might be pregnant? I've been dreaming about this moment for a year and now that it might really be happening I can't quite take it in. It feels so unreal.

Well what did you expect, a visit from the angels?, I chide myself.

I feel surrounded by a magic aura and I'm surprised no one else can tell. I want to be cool about this, keep it to myself for now. Peter won't notice that my monthly mood swings are delayed.

It's no good, I have to tell someone. I call my friend Georgy on some pretence and blurt out my suspicions. She giggles, it's so exciting. She is already an auntie many times over, but this time it's me, a friend, a peer, having a baby. Forever practical she takes over and offers to arrange an appointment with her GP to have it confirmed, knowing that I only see my own frequently inebriated local GP when I absolutely have to. How will I announce the happy tidings to Peter? If there are happy tidings to impart that is. I play the possible scene over and over in my head, borrowing from every book, every film, and every soap opera I've ever watched. I picture myself basking in this wonderful glow of having achieved something so clever, so wonderful, it brings tears to my eyes. Pathetic really, but nice.

Georgy's Dr. Barnes can see me the next day and while he takes some blood we have a little chat about this and that. I tell him my breasts feel sore, and that I need the loo at least twice as much as normal. Mind you, I'm also drinking quite a lot as they say it's good for the baby. I get the feeling that Dr. Barnes is not really listening to me jabbering on. I suppose the biggest thing that has happened to me since Peter arrived on the scene isn't that exciting for him. Then he tells me that he will call on Tuesday if there is a pregnancy to confirm. And with that, I'm out of the door. I feel a little deflated. I just wish he could have been a little more excited. It seems that even a positive result doesn't mean anything until I make it to three months. As if a pregnancy before that deadline is somehow not quite to be taken seriously. Anyway, I'm sure I'm already getting a huge bulge. And sticking my belly forward I walk down Harley Street dreaming about my new life as a mother.

On Tuesday I stay in the office waiting by the phone all day and not a bleep. I'm scared, just imagine they've lost the sample, or they've found out I'm suffering from some dreadful disease. All day I think of nothing else. I'm in a complete daze and my work only serves as an unwelcome distraction from what is truly important here. Anyway, who cares, soon I'll be on maternity leave. Well, soonish.

By four the phone still hasn't rung and I decide to pick up the phone myself.

"Ah, Lysanne, your sample results are indeed back, I believe congratulations are in order."

The nurse's voice is friendly and warm. I mumble something to her, gently put down the receiver and punch the air as I do a triple swerve in my swivel chair. I just can't believe it. I'm really pregnant. After only four months of trying I'm really pregnant. Never mind all the bad stories about some medical drug my mother took when she was expecting me, I'm really and truly pregnant. I quickly clear my desk of some urgent work and then I'm on my way home to tell Peter. Sitting in the back of the cab I play the scene over and over in my head. I'll pass him the wine and say, "in eight months time we'll be toasting with champagne". He'll look at me and say, "do you mean what I think you mean.....", and then he'll come around to my side of the table encouraged by the biggest smile he has ever seen. He'll take me in his arms and whisper romantic things in my ear, after which he'll kneel down and look adoringly at my tummy. That's the plan, anyway.

Dinner is burned, I'm in a heap, and Peter is mopping up canned lobster soup from a sticky kitchen floor. I'm in tears. You might say the announcement didn't go as planned. It started off with Peter calling to say he would be late. I shouted down the phone that he couldn't treat his baby like this. Not quite fair since he doesn't yet know he's having one. Thankfully, the mobile network was at breaking point and he yelled back, "I love you too baby, see you in a little while." A little while becomes three hours, by which time I'm almost asleep, courtesy of the pregnancy hormones.

When I wake up from my snooze I see him making a sandwich in the kitchen.

"No, no, no!"

I get him to sit down at the dinner table and re-light the candles, or what's left of them. Poor guy, he knows something is up, but he hasn't got a clue.

"Are you okay? I'm sorry I'm late, these bloody editors you know....."

"No, I'm fine...", and then, not having the greatest of co-ordination skills anyway, least of all with hormones raging through my body and multiplying by the second, I drop the soup. Soup, stress, joy, hormones, disappointment, all come crashing to the floor with a loud bang, with me in the middle, a howling heap of womanhood.

"Anyone would think you're pregnant the way you're carrying on."

More howls from the kitchen floor. He gradually manages to make sense of what I'm saying in between the hiccups and the snorts. A howling heap on the floor is not quite the picture of capable motherhood I had planned to present.

Later, all cuddled up in bed he whispers, "I'm really proud of you", and he puts his hand on my tummy. I put my hand over his and as we fall asleep I feel a rush of contentment and security. It didn't turn out too bad after all.

We decide to tell our respective parents at once and I so much want to be able to nip around the corner and tell them over a quiet cup of tea. However, with the North Sea between us that is not an option, and though I don't want to tell them over the phone, I make the best of it. I'm due in June, right around the time of their wedding anniversary, and so I drop into the conversation that I might, might just have a very special anniversary present for them. Mamma guesses immediately and overcome with grandmotherly emotion she passes the phone straight to my father, who, realising what's going on, is no less overcome.

Then the yelps and exclamations of joy take over and we all agree that we wish we lived closer to each other, so we could have a proper celebration. In the evening I'm still feeling a little sad and homesick so Peter suggests I try and fix a trip over to Holland in the next few weeks. It's terribly sweet of him, but I don't really know if it's possible. Is it safe to fly?

In a way this pregnancy is as important to mamma as it is to me. She suffered two miscarriages between the birth of my brother and myself. When she was pregnant with me there was a new 'miracle' drug on the market which was supposed to help the pregnancy snuggle more tightly into the lining of the womb. Years later it became apparent that this drug, abbreviated to DES, actually affected the development of foetus adversely, and that a large number of daughters as well as sons suffered reproductive problems. When I was about eighteen years old there was a whole spate of stories in the Dutch press about this scandal. Mamma and I went to a DES-clinic in Holland a few months before the wedding only to be told to wait and see what happens. I know how worried she has been and how guilty she feels about having taken this drug. I might tell her a hundred times that it wasn't her fault, but only a healthy pregnancy will make the real difference.

On Sunday I'm off to church on my own as usual. Peter has tried from time to time to get involved in the churchy bit of my life, but it just isn't his thing. After a brief spell where I deemed it my responsibility to convert him to a spiritual life, I was wisely told to back off by Martin, our local priest, and leave him alone to find his own path in life. After the service there is a jumble sale for the Homeless Unit, and I intend to buy something for the baby. First I light a candle in the chapel and say a big thank you for this pregnancy and ask for its protection. I imagine myself growing bigger and bigger over the next few months as I help out with the after service coffee. I run into Simon, one of the other coffee servers, and brimming over with enthusiasm I tell him my news.

"How far gone are you?" he asks.

"Eight weeks."

"Well, it's early days then, but good luck anyway."

What a killjoy. Relegated again to the not yet three months pregnant brigade I quickly find someone else to tell, and from her I get the cuddle and the positive reaction I want. I buy a little white knitted cardigan. After all, I'll be helping the homeless unit at St. Martin's by buying it, and it will surely carry a blessing for the baby.

On my way home I pop into the bookshop and buy two books on pregnancy and one on childbirth. After a few glances at the ghastly birth scenes I decide to keep the latter locked away for now. Yuck. Mamma says that by the time you reach the end of your pregnancy you don't care how it comes out, you just want it out! The wisdom of Mother Nature I suppose. I know I would like to give birth in the bath, the only place I feel comfortable when period pains have me doubled up in agony. Can contractions be worse?

In two weeks time I'm going home to see my parents. I'm a little concerned because I read this article which says that flying in early pregnancy can cause miscarriages, but as Peter points out, pregnant stewardesses seem to cope. Or do they stop working as soon as they test positive. I think not. Yet, what is disturbing is that I keep coming across this stuff about miscarriages. I suppose that being pregnant I'm extra sensitive to it, but it really does annoy me.

Only four more weeks and I'm in the clear.

Ten weeks, and Georgy and I meet up for some sushi to celebrate the fact that I'm a quarter of the way through my pregnancy. Well, we don't need much of an excuse to have a feast. I tell her that Peter has been joking about the film '9$\frac{1}{2}$' weeks, and that he makes sly comments about certain activities portrayed therein. I know that sex is not dangerous to the baby, but already I'm not so sure.

My whole body is changing. Apart from being sore as hell, my breasts no longer feel the focal points of sexual attraction they used to be. Peter tries to be sympathetic, but he fears the next ten years without sex, not a happy prospect. Georgy knows someone who went off sex for a whole year after giving birth, as well as during her pregnancy. We decide to keep that bit of information from Peter for now. She says I already look different, that my face has a glow. I know she is probably just saying it to please me, but I love it.

I order double the amount of sushi, the excuse being that I'm now eating for two. I've started talking to my tummy, as well as keeping this diary. Still feel a little bit uncomfortable though, as if I'm tempting fate. After dinner I lean back on the floor of the restaurant like a bloated elephant. I completely overdid it with the eating for two. I go home and lie down on the bed, images of a little foetus stuffing its face with sushi milling around in my head.

Mamma rings to check what time I'll be arriving tomorrow. She also has another bit of unexpected news. My cousin Pamela is also expecting a baby, and she is due in June! Pam and I have always had a lot in common and we got married the same year. It's great fun to hear that we're taking this next step on the path to mature parenthood together. I immediately call her and we have a long chat comparing morning sickness symptoms and pain relief methods. She is already really well read up on the pain relief bit, but I'm too Dutch to even consider the topic. Dutch women tend to give birth at home with as little intervention as possible. Just think, our due dates are only two weeks apart, we may even deliver our babies on the same day.

Tomorrow's flight only takes 45 minutes and I'm sure that can't be long enough to do any damage. I've had a slight sensation of tenderness in my tummy, ever since that sushi binge, but I suppose that's to do with the uterus growing and things moving around in there. It's quite amazing how your body just seems to take over and know exactly what to do. Like a software programme rolling out in its own good time, to an unseen timetable.

At the airport I make a fuss because I don't trust the scanner. They reassure me it's fine and become totally fed up with me for not wanting to believe them. In the end they let me go around it, but not without a jolly good frisk down. I sit by the window and tell my tummy that we're on our way to opa and oma, Dutch for granny and granddad. Part of me knows I'm being totally pathetic and the other part of me happily dreams her daydreams and imagines taking this flight in little more than six months time with a real life baby strapped onto my lap. My daydreams do not yet include inconsolably screaming babies or dirty nappies, only bliss and happy families.

My parents meet me at Rotterdam airport. Mamma holds me as if I'm made of bone china, whereas Pappa gives me the usual bear hug and a little extra squeeze for good luck. "Voorzichtig", admonishes mamma, which means 'be careful'. We have a lovely weekend together and all too soon we are back at the airport and saying our goodbye's. I had the feeling that mamma thought we'd been a little too premature in telling everyone about the pregnancy, and I suppose after suffering miscarriages like she did you do tend to want to be more careful. I just love all the attention and the kudos and I can't see how it would jeopardise the pregnancy whether you tell people or not. Let the Greeks get hung up on hubris, I think it's just plain common sense.

As we say our farewells I swallow away this huge lump in my throat. I feel quite vulnerable and I hate saying goodbye to the two people who have brought me up to be strong and independent yet allow me to be their little girl when I need to.

Back home I go into organising mode. Ever since Peter's company moved from Camden to Uxbridge he's slowly been going mad sitting in traffic jams. A ten minute bicycle ride to work has turned into a car journey of an hour there and back again, most of it stuck in the unmoveable mass that is the North Circular. So in order to ensure at least one sane parent for this baby we have decided to move out to the suburbs as well, probably in April. By then I'll be about halfway through the pregnancy. I don't really want to start my ante-natal care in one place and then change to another, although realise I have no clue what I mean when I talk about ante-natal care.

One of the girls at work mentioned that her hospital runs a domino scheme for midwives. Not one midwife after the other falling over drunk, which is what it conjured up in my brain, but a single midwife who follows you through your pregnancy right up to the birth. If I want something like that I can't be changing health authorities halfway through and so I had better find out where and how I can register.

Almost there, only one more week to go and trimester two here I come!

Peter has started calling me his pregno, a term of endearment if ever I heard one. I'm talking more and more to my tummy and sometimes lie awake at night caressing that part of my belly where I think the baby is. I check its progress in my books, and it's really starting to look like a baby now. I run various names by Peter, which he finds terribly irritating, and make lists at the back of my diary. I haven't felt nauseous at all these past few weeks, I actually didn't even feel that sick in the beginning. My breasts are less sore, and I only visit the toilet often because I'm still drinking a lot.

There is a nagging voice at the back of my head which says something is wrong. Why am I not feeling pregnant anymore? I hush up the little voice and remind myself that I'll soon be going into the second trimester, and that it's normal for the early symptoms to stop. But even my week-by-week baby book seems part of the conspiracy. Between the eleventh and the twelfth week there is a whole section about miscarriage. Damn it, I keep opening it up on that page. One moment I'm happy as Larry, and the next I'm fretting my little heart out, seeing bad omens everywhere and wishing we hadn't told everyone now. What's wrong?

I ignore the nagging doubts and do what I do best by getting to work on the ante-natal aspect of the move. Peter has borrowed the Uxbridge Yellow Pages from work and I get on the phone to local GP's to plan my maternity care.

It's strange, the more I hear myself talking about being pregnant, the more I feel it slipping away from me. It also turns out to be hopelessly difficult just to get someone to grasp the fact that we will be moving halfway through the pregnancy and that all I want is to have continuity in my maternity care. All they are interested in is whether we have a house yet and whether it's in their catchment area. Most of them don't even want to bother, they just tell me to talk to my current GP. Finally I get through to Dr. Walker's surgery. A very understanding and clearly more intelligent than average receptionist hears me out. She realises the dilemma, and puts me on hold while she talks to the doctor. Bingo! He suggests they take me on for maternity care only, and then, once we have moved out to the area, Peter and I, and of course, Junior, as Peter has started to refer to our baby, will be registered as 'full' patients. It seems a wonderful solution and we make an appointment for the first ante natal check in two weeks time.

Wow, maternity care, ante natal clinic.... it all sounds so real, I'm finally getting there.

Up .... and down ...... we're fighting. I'm tearful and I'm irrational. I feel more irrational than before a period. I just want to cry all the time. People tell me it's normal for pregnant women to be so wobbly, but it's something else. Ever since I've known about DES I've been afraid that having a family might not be as straightforward for me as it seems to be for others. Then we start trying, we fall pregnant within months, and it is almost too good to be true.

Yes, that's how I feel. It's too good to be true. Someone, somewhere, is suddenly going to pull the rabbit out of the hat, or rather, put the rabbit back in the hat, and say it was all a big joke. How could I have been so stupid, so proud, to believe I could actually be pregnant?

My mood confuses Peter. First he gets a bit annoyed and tells me to pull myself together. On the other hand, I'm frightening him, since he knows my instincts are usually right. We're both exhausted and since we can't make sense of the situation we go to bed. Peter puts his arm around me and lays his hand on my tummy, just as he has done every night in the past weeks.

"Don't worry, everything will be fine," he whispers, but I'm not so sure.

Chapter 2

NO LONGER PREGNANT

It's six in the morning. I've just been to the toilet and I'm bleeding. I'm sitting on the sofa wrapped in a big sweater. My first concern is that I don't have any sanitary towels. I slung them all out two months ago expecting to be done with periods for the next nine months. My tummy hurts, a low nagging ache, not even a real cramp. This is all wrong. I'm scared.

I smoke one of Peter's cigarettes out the tiny kitchen window and then go back to bed to try and fall asleep again. Maybe if I go back to sleep it will all turn out to have been a nightmare. I don't wake Peter, not yet. I put both hands over my tummy and pray for my pregnancy and for myself. Surely God wouldn't let anything happen to this baby?

I toss and turn and find that I can't go back to sleep. I nudge Peter awake. I tell him I'm bleeding.

"Is that bad?" he mumbles, still half asleep. Now I shake him until he is wide awake. Well, I'm suffering, he might as well suffer too. He asks what he can do, and goes out to buy some sanitary towels and painkillers. I don't know if I should take anything for the pain. Perhaps I need to know what I'm feeling, so that I can describe it to the doctor. What if I pass the baby?

Peter returns from his errand with Co-Op Super Size, shaped like bricks, and makes me a cup of tea. He says everything will be all right. For him maybe, but not for me. I want to call mamma but I feel such an idiot. Yet she is probably the person who understands me better than anyone else and she is also in a position to give me advice.

At eight I call her. She says to call the doctor, and not to be too pessimistic. She also had a bleed when pregnant with my brother, and sometimes it just means you need to take it easy for a bit. As always I feel reassured by her.

Reluctantly I call my regular GP. The receptionist tells me to come in during normal surgery hours. I tell her I won't, not on her advice. I tell her I want to speak to the doctor. She will try to get a locum to call me back and I assume 'Dr. Alchy' has been out on the binge last night. Peter suggests I call Dr. Walker, but I don't want to, I'm still his maternity patient, and I want to keep that status a little longer. I wait for the locum to call. The minutes are ticking by so slowly, and I'm impatient. Peter hovers around with tea and toast, but I'm not hungry. Then finally the phone goes.

"Keep warm, put your feet up, and wait and see for a few days. If your pregnancy is going to terminate itself there is nothing we can do about it anyway."

What an awful thing to say. I push his words out of my mind. I can't sit around waiting to see, I need action, I need to know what's happening!

Peter has gone off to work. There is nothing else he can do, and his hovering helplessness just gets on my nerves. He keeps saying it will be okay. But it's not okay, it's not okay at all. He's bought me all kinds of munchies, and it reminds me of what he does when I have my periods. Chocolate bars, toffees, a hot water bottle ... but I don't want to be reminded of periods.

Georgy promises to come round later today, and asks me whether I want to speak to a friend of hers who had a miscarriage last year. I take down her friend's number but I won't call yet. I'm not having a miscarriage, am I?

Now it's just me, daytime television, and this terrible, terrible sense of foreboding. Maybe I shouldn't have had all that sushi. Maybe I shouldn't have flown. Or maybe that crazy confused mix of hubris and Calvinist moralising last night wasn't just the result of a feverish brain. Where did I go wrong? I try and doze a bit but I'm bursting to go to the loo. I don't dare. What if I've lost more blood. I just try and lie very still under my duvet in front of the television.

It's no use. I can't hold my wee for the next six months. Finally I just have to go, the pain of my swollen bladder worse than the cramps. I take a deep breath. Why the hell did I buy pink flowery toilet paper? I think it was clear though. I call my mother. She thinks that's a good sign.

I try to sleep again. I can't sleep. I hold myself like a baby. I feel so alone, so frightened. Praying doesn't help either. Didn't get what I asked for anyway, or maybe I did. Maybe I was never supposed to have a baby, maybe this is God's way of getting the message through.

Georgy calls, she's running late. Peter calls, he will be home later this afternoon. Mamma calls again, but there's not much to say. It's great to have all these loving people around me, but inside I'm empty. Something inside me has died, is dead, is very dead. I can feel it now, I know it, and it makes me unbearably sad. This is the end. Inside me there is no more hope, and I pound the mattress with my fists in a mad rage howling like a child at the unfairness of it all. Finally I weep quietly and accept that I've lost my pregnancy.

Exhausted from this outburst of emotion I'm now ready for some tough answers. I admit to myself that this is the end, and call Dr. Walker, my maternity only Dr. Walker. The kind receptionist once again hears me out, and I thank God for her ability to listen. She asks me to call back later, when Dr. Walker is between surgery and house calls.

I spend the half hour dozing as best I can and by the time I call back I'm eerily calm and business like. Dr. Walker realises my need to know exactly what's going on and we make an appointment for the next day. I zap through all the crappy satellite channels and try to avoid any pictures of nappies or babies. That turns out to be an impossible task and I turn over and just stare at the wall. I'm deadly tired.

Georgy arrives with a bunch of flowers and half the inventory of the M&S food halls. She keeps me company until Peter comes home. Then gives him a big hug and goes on her way. Now we're alone, really alone. No Junior to laugh and joke about, no names to annoy each other with, no plans for the future. Just fears for the next day. I'm so terribly scared, especially about passing the baby in the night. Peter is fantastic in terms of looking after me and trying to cheer me up, but it's not good enough. I miss his grief, where are his tears? He cooks me his *piece de resistance*, creamy carbonara pasta. Halfway through dinner he takes my hand and says that he knows everything will turn out fine. What he means is that we were perfectly happy before we were expecting, and that if this is the end of this pregnancy, we could still be happy being just the two of us again.

Happy? Happier??? Is that what he means. It's the last thing I want to hear. I need to see him to cry for his own loss, not see it as my loss, trying to be strong for me. I want to cry together, to mourn our lost pregnancy, together. I'm disappointed and I wonder if he actually cares. Perhaps he is relieved. I try not to show my feelings, but I sit through dinner completely morose. Peter is being practical, planning the next day. It takes 45 minutes to drive to the new office, so Dr. Walker is about 40 minutes away.

"I'll drop you off........", dagger looks from me, "unless you want me to stay of course." Of course he'll stay, he's just worried it's a woman kind of thing. No place for him. I am so confused and angry inside, but I won't let it out.

He falls asleep beside me and I feel completely alone. Alone with my sadness, alone with our loss.

The next morning we end up leaving the house fifteen minutes late, a disaster for someone like me who usually turns up half an hour early. All I can do is bitch. The traffic is worse than normal. I take all my hurt and anger out on Peter. I blame him for our late start, for choosing the wrong route, and for anything else I can think of. I know I'm being unfair, but I can't help it. I feel like a failure, and so I want him to feel like a failure too. It's bad enough going to see my maternity care doctor for a very non-maternity care reason. And now this failed pregno, is a late failed pregno, and it's all Peter's fault.

By the time we get there we are only ten minutes late and the kind receptionist asks us to go and wait in the waiting room. It's a world apart from what I'm used to in our North London practice. For a start, it's clean and fresh, with notices on the walls and plants in the windows.

Meeting Dr. Walker in person is strange. I want to thank him for taking me on as a maternity patient, but what maternity? Thanks for taking on this failure, who made such a song and dance about being pregnant and now comes here un-pregnant like a deflated balloon. He feels my belly and says it's the right size for almost thirteen weeks. He takes out a gadget and says it's to hear the heartbeat. I didn't even know they could do that. He moves it across my belly and finds a lot of whooshing noises, but no heartbeat. Then he says it's quite usual not to hear the heartbeat at this stage, which is confusing, but I'm not bleeding anymore which he thinks is a good sign. We hang on his every word.

"Do you think Lysanne might still be pregnant then?" Peter tries to get some clarity.

"The best way to tell is to have a scan. I'll refer you on to the local hospital and they will take a better look." But then, on the way out he adds: "Sometimes a miscarriage is God's way of saying that things weren't right with the baby." I don't know if he says it because he's spotted the little cross I wear, but I think to myself that if that's the way God works He could do with a more efficient production manager. Peter calls work to tell them he is going to be in even later. We don't know if we're coming or going. I feel guilty Peter is having to take so much time off for me, although they are all very understanding. I feel a lot less guilty about my own work. There's a recording in the afternoon which I know he can't miss, and so I enjoy having him with me for now, and try not to worry about the rest of the day.

As we drive the three miles to the hospital I'm swung between hope and despair. Surely Dr. Walker wouldn't send us to the hospital for a scan if there wasn't some remote chance. I try not to think about my total conviction yesterday that it was all over. Perhaps it was just me being negative, giving up before there was any reason to. I quietly apologise to my baby and then I feel like a complete idiot again.

We head for Radiography. After all, that's where Dr. Walker said they would do the scan. There are two heavily pregnant women waiting outside the radiographers' room. Both reading 'Mother & Baby' magazine. There seems to be no reception, and we don't really know what to do. I will Peter to be strong and to take charge, but he is too used to me being the bossy one. Finally I knock on the door with 'RADIOGRAPHY' written on it. A nurse sticks out her head, grabs Dr. Walker's piece of paper and disappears. Then she is back. "We don't really admit emergency cases here, but we'll see you anyway."

Well thank you very much, I already feel such an idiot, now I feel like a bloody nuisance as well.

"We weren't quite sure...," Peter adds feebly.

"Is your bladder full?" this directed at me, not Peter. "We can't scan you without a full bladder you know." I've screwed up again. How was I to know about the full bladder.

"Your doctor should have told you," and with that I get a glass and a two litre jug of water handed to me. Like a good girl I start drinking, and drinking, as if to make up for being such a bloody nuisance. By the time we are called in, about an hour later, my bladder is fit to burst. A nurse shows me where to take off my trousers and underwear and tells me to lie down on the bed. Then a woolly blanket is draped over my lower half. This is for modesty's sake I suppose, though by now I couldn't have cared less. Peter sits beside me and holds my

26

hand. He is as bewildered as I am. I can only see part of the screen, but as I crane my neck to see more the radiographer turns the screen away from me.

"I can't really see anything. Hum, maybe your bladder is too full."

She can't see anything, what does that mean, she can't see a baby, or she can't see the abdominal area, or what? I wish she was clearer. She tells me to go and empty my bladder, but only a little. Try that when you're holding down five pints of water. But I try and do everything as best I can. I want to show that I'm trying hard to do things right. Maybe that way I can make things be right again.

I'm back on the bed, blanket pulled up, gel on my tummy, and this time the screen is turned right away from us.

"Do you see anything now?" I ask, finding the wait unbearable.

"Well actually, there is no baby there, there is a sack, but no foetus. Did you pass any clots when you started bleeding?"

It takes me a moment to realise that by clots she means bits of baby.

"No, I've been really scared of that happening, but there has been nothing at all."

"Then there was probably never a baby in the first place," she says, switching off the monitor with a flick. I look at Peter.

"You mean my wife was never pregnant to begin with?"

"Oh yes, she was definitely pregnant. Your wife has what is called an empty sack, or in medical terms, a blighted ovum. It's not unusual in a first pregnancy. The cells making the baby probably never made it beyond the first week, and really, your wife should have miscarried much sooner."

Okay, I know she doesn't mean it like that, but it's like being told I can't even miscarry properly! In actual fact I feel quite proud that my poor body tried to hang on to it for so long.

"So it wasn't a phantom pregnancy?"

Thank you Peter. Thanks for making me out to be a raving lunatic as well as a complete failure at motherhood.

"No, as I said, your wife was certainly pregnant, and now we have to give her a scrape so that she doesn't get any infections. Nurse here will take you up to the ward and explain." And with that, she moves out to another room, and despite her attempt at friendliness I hear her think ... next.

Give me a scrape, clear me out. I don't know what it means but it sounds pretty awful. And I'm going to have to stay the night at the hospital. The last time I was in hospital I was four years old. We weren't expecting to be admitted and I tell the nurse that I don't have a nighty with me. Not that I usually wear a nighty, I'm not even sure I own one. She says I can borrow one from the hospital and for the operation I will need to wear a special gown anyway.

I'm taken up to Kennedy, the gynaecological ward, where I'm shown into a room with three other beds. The curtains are drawn around two of the beds, and I can hear someone sobbing. I make myself comfortable on the fourth bed, closest to the door, and I realise that I feel perversely at home in this environment. Maybe it has something to do with watching so many episodes of 'Casualty'.

Peter gives me a hug and hurries off to do his recording. He's late, as usual, but this time it was to be with me, and I am thankful for that.

I'm no longer in pain, but I do feel sick with emotion and exhaustion. The nurses help me get settled and their care and attention make me feel very looked after. They explain that I will be given a general anaesthetic, before they clean me out. The operation is called a dilatation and curettage, or D&C for short. Dilating the cervix, which means stretching it so they can get the instruments through, and scraping away the lining of the womb. Ouch!

I'm rapidly learning the medical terminology. Bits of baby are referred to as matter or clots. A miscarriage, is an abortion, an incomplete miscarriage a missed abortion, and women who have regular miscarriages are frequent aborters. I wonder if they earn air-miles, like frequent flyers.

Though none of the nursing staff use these terms, I overhear doctors who do, and I wonder if they realise how painful and downright confusing this is. There are two women in the smoking room talking about the fact that there are cases on our ward who are in for abortions, but they might well have overheard the doctors talking about miscarriages. I bum a cigarette off one of them and take grim satisfaction in treating my body with the same disdain it seems to be treating me.

Back on the ward the girl behind the curtain just cries and cries. I lie back and close my eyes, I feel too empty to cry. From time to time the nurses pop their head around the door to see if we're okay. Despite being rushed off their feet, they're really lovely.

The anaesthetist arrives at my bedside and asks me if I'm allergic to anything. I mention the asthma in my family, but can't come up with anything better than that. I have this ridiculous need to please everybody, to be a model patient. Of course my surgery can be postponed if the surgeons have to perform a Caesarean first. Crazy thing is, the woman having the Caesarean probably feels she's unlucky, yet I would swap places with her any day.

How we compare our misfortunes ...

Peter comes to see me just before I go down to theatre. I ask how the recording went but really I couldn't care less. I feel so weak, so vulnerable. I don't see that he is confused too, having had to call his parents, mine, our closest friends, all with the sad news of the miscarriage.

He brings a huge basket of flowers from his colleagues at work, for the both of us. I leave him standing there with his huge basket of flowers in his hands looking a complete misery. How dare he be miserable, I'm the one on my way down to theatre. Alone, completely alone.

I'm wheeled down the corridor on my bed. For a born control freak like me it's scary to be so completely at other people's mercy. I have no more control over my life than a child. And yet, part of me feels as vulnerable as a child so that it seems right just to let them take over. Holding all these mixed feelings exhausts me. Relief that the cause of all the pain and fear of the last 24 hours has been found and sadness at the loss of my pregnancy. I close my eyes. My chart has been perched on my tummy, and I worry that it might fall off. Oh what the hell, it's not my concern. I wish I could close my ears to the innate chattering going on over my head. Then it's down in the elevator, with patients and visitors staring at me as I go past. I am a nothing, a patient, a bundle on a bed, empty as a corpse.

Through the round windows in the doors I see the operating theatre. I feel scared and alone. The anaesthetist puts his needle into my hand and it stings.

"No it doesn't hurt," I tell him. Brave little girl that I am.

Then as he tells me to count backwards from ten the whole world disappears.

Oblivion.

"It hurts, Oh God it hurts." I'm trying to be brave but I'm in agony. My entire lower half feels on fire. Like one massive cramp. I'm dazed. I try to get someone's attention. I have this weird feeling that I've not existed for the past hours or even days. I've lost a whole segment of time.

I'm told I'm in the recovery room and I realise I have an oxygen mask on my face. Why? Has something gone wrong? I've no idea how long I've been gone. I am confused, scared, and in such terrible pain. Why isn't anyone doing anything to help me? I feel abandoned, wham bam thank you ma'm, operation over, patient cleared out. I try not to be a nuisance, but bloody hell, it hurts. Instinctively I try and struggle up so that I can hunch over to minimise the pain.

"You can't do that. Lie down," a nurse snaps. Now I've got their attention.

"Then please give me something for the pain."

Finally someone pushes a needle into my arm. They tell me it will start working in a few minutes. It doesn't. It still hurts as I'm being wheeled back upstairs onto the ward where it is very quiet. It's past midnight and everyone is asleep. I'm parked in my own bay, and the curtains are drawn. Peter has patiently been waiting for me to come back up.

He grabs my hand where the anaesthetist's needle still protrudes.

"Au!"

He lets go, and looks at me with loving, questioning eyes. "What can I do?"

I can't help him.

I need the help.

I'm angry, sad, and yet in a strange way, also relieved.

It's all over. I can go home.

I can start again. We can start again.

We can put it all behind us.

Chapter 3

BACK TO NORMAL?

I leave the hospital the next day. The pain in my tummy has gone but my legs feel like I've been riding bareback across the Rocky Mountains. It comes to me with a jolt. The image of myself, out cold, legs in stirrups, helpless on an operating table. It's not exactly my pretty face they've been staring at either. I'm no prude, but the thought makes me feel dirty, exposed. I push the image away, that is something I just can't deal with right now.

June, the ward sister hands me some information about miscarriages. The flyer tells you about losing blood for a few more days, feeling a bit wobbly, and if miscarrying late in pregnancy, leaking breasts. Great, I'm lucky to be spared those then I suppose. There are also some help numbers on the back, national as well as local.

"Don't be afraid to ask for help," says June on the way out, "you'll have so many emotions to deal with, and there are people who can help you with them."

I'm embarrassed to take the papers. Oh, terribly grateful and all that, but I'm not likely to go and ask for help, am I? I'm the help giver, always have been. The one that copes and gets on with things. I'm strong, I cope, and don't tell me I won't. I bury the papers at the very bottom of my bag.

"Hi darling, looking good!"

Peter arrives to pick me up and is back to his everyday self. I'm not, I'm reluctant to leave the relative safety of the hospital. Here I was sick. Here it was recognised, at least by most, that I'd been through something really sad. Here I was safe, wrapped in a cocoon. In comparison, the outside world is bleak, and full of the realities of normal life. And quite frankly, it scares me to death.

In the car I sit very still. I watch the fields whizzing by and I feel disconnected. Unconsciously I rest my hand on my belly, as I did so many times in the past weeks. I quickly take my hand away, there's nothing there now, it's empty. The tiny gesture brings the tears welling up in my eyes.

At home I don't want to get out of the car. I'm scared. I don't feel ready. I don't want Peter, my friends, my colleagues, or anyone else, to think that I'm back to normal again. I remember a character in a book who, after losing her husband, spent six months in bed with the covers pulled over her head. A self-imposed retreat from the world, in order to mourn. It's what I want to do, but can't do. What choice do I have but to go with a heavy tread up the three flights of stairs to our apartment. Peter follows behind with my bag. He's taken the white knitted cardigan and the pregnancy books away and put them in the loft. I hold his hand, and thank him for being so considerate. Then I walk to the long mirror where I last stood naked, imagining my unborn baby doing summersaults in my tummy.

I feel robbed. Robbed of that special feeling that being pregnant bestows on you. Robbed of that little spark that had become my constant companion. I feel such an idiot. I feel tricked as if someone has played this almighty sick practical joke on me. And I'm furious with God.

What a mess.

Peter has been booked out on a shoot for the rest of the week, and so I go and spend some time with pappa and mamma. I've only talked to them once on the phone, and I really feel in need of some additional cuddles and looking after. The taxi driver wants to know if I'm going somewhere nice. Being very Dutch, and so rather forthright, I tell him that I'm going home to my mum and dad because I've just had a miscarriage.

"I'm sorry for you dear," he says, and I can see that he means it. "My wife and I have three children, guess we're just lucky." And for want of a better topic, he goes on to tell me all about them, including the one who has the first grandchild on the way. I stare out of the window, watching the fields along the North Circular whizzing by in the opposite direction from yesterday. I don't let him see my tears. I won't let anyone see my tears.

At the check-in desk I'm joined in the line by a heavily pregnant woman. I change queues, but still my eyes are drawn to her again and again. I see them everywhere now, as if the whole world is pregnant except for me. As I go through security to board the plane I remember the fuss I made coming through the security gates last time. I imagine the security guard giving me a 'serves you right' look. Sheer paranoia, but it hurts. *Oh stop it Lysanne*, I feel too sorry for myself, I shouldn't be feeling so sorry for myself. *There are worse things in life Lysanne*, I tell myself in the voice of my upbringing, *read your paper. War in Asia, famine in Africa, a hijacked train. So what's your problem?* My problem is that I am trying to deny I have a problem while expecting everyone else around me to respect the fact that I do. Talk about mixed messages!

I remember the daydreams I had on the way out to Holland only three weeks ago. Don't cry, not here, not on the plane. The lump in my throat hurts so much. I swallow down the tears. I feel such an idiot, I feel such a fool. My brother collects me from the airport and gives me a big hug.

"Hé Sanne," he says, as he holds me tight.

My parents are waiting for me at the door. They pull me inside and sit me down on the sofa. Pappa has bought all my favourite Dutch food, and mamma looks at me, her grey eyes full of love and concern. I nourish myself with their love. It's good to be home. They all comment on how brave I am.

Am I brave, or just stupid?

Perhaps the reality of what's happened just hasn't sunk in. But it's not that, it's just that I'm eager to please and I know the rules of the game. After all, wasn't it my maternal grandfather who wrote in a poem to my mother; when times are hard, remember to be tough and strong, because weak is cowardly.

So I say bravely: "Wasn't meant to be, nature's way."

My parents nod, other people nod, relieved I'm taking it so well.

I try to put a brave face on it, as much to protect them as to protect myself. I've no idea when and if I would want to start trying again, but I tell them it's good to know I could fall pregnant so easily. I wallow in the luxury of being back under the parental umbrella for a while, and it gives me the same secure feeling as the hospital did.

All too soon it's time for me to fly back home to England. I can't stay the child. I am an adult, I have responsibilities, work, a mortgage to pay. Yep, it's back to life as normal again, and I pick up the thread as best I can.

At St. Martin's I run into Simon, the coffee server who had seemed so indifferent to the news of my pregnancy. "We missed you last week."

I fill him in, upon which Simon tells me that he and his wife have already suffered two miscarriages. He is one of the few people who doesn't try to make it right for me. He just gives me a big hug and says that Peter and I can always come and talk to them if we feel the need.

Selfish, selfish, me. I never gave it a second thought as I was going around announcing my big news. How it must have hurt people for whom getting pregnant and having a baby does not speak for itself. If I'm learning anything from this, it's a little more discretion for my own and, more so, for other people's sake.

With Simon I feel for the first time I can show my true feelings, my disappointment, my hurt pride, my pain. Normally I'm scared to be pitied, and can't take on board much concern and sympathy. So I put up this façade. After all, this is me remember; Ms. Cheerful Smile on her Face, Always Game for a Laugh. The fact of the matter is, I don't know how to be anything other. I want people to talk about it, to acknowledge something pretty awful has happened to us, and on the other hand I want to show that I'm strong and capable. Simon reads the confusion in my face, "Just look after yourself will you, you'll need it."

It's been a month now since the miscarriage and my period arrives, bang on time, 28 days after the D&C. There is something deeply reassuring about it. At least the whole system is up and running again. Period cramps and all. The hot water bottle is out, and so are the chocolate bars. Not that it helps much.

Out in the street the Christmas preparations are in full swing. Shop windows are decorated, carols piped through every shop and street, yet I can't seem to get into the mood at all. In fact, I can't wait for it to be over this year. On the way home from a Swedish Christmas party I bite Peter's head off for asking why I was so quiet. As if he hadn't noticed there were at least three pregnant women in the room.

"What do you mean, what's wrong," I snap, "I lost a bloody baby remember?"

Pathetic, pathetic. Completely over the top, but I score a double whammy anyway. One, you seem to have forgotten your own lost fatherhood. And two, you are an uncaring bastard who doesn't love me enough to understand how I feel.

Unfair, totally unfair. He's been so supportive, has tried to help me as best he can. Why isn't he hurting though. Why can't he have moments of deep sadness like I do. It really makes me wonder if he actually wanted this pregnancy?

I'm so self-absorbed and I hate myself for what I'm thinking and saying. But I'm like a hurt animal, lashing out at anything and everything that tries to get close. What I want more than anything is a hug, and yet I won't let anyone near me. I might fall apart, drop the façade, and lose it completely. Control freak from birth, I'm now in the running for the Guinness Book of Records.

If I hear one more word about baby Jesus I'll explode. Why couldn't I have miscarried just before Easter, at least the general mood would have been either one of secular indifference, or spiritual soberness. Yet now all is jollity, festivity, happy families, and we are not. Am I becoming too self-indulgent in my grief? Surely, it's been six weeks now, shouldn't I be getting over it. Earlier this afternoon, one of the old ladies came up to me at church and asked me how the baby was doing. Hell, what could I say.

"It's not.... I mean.... it's gone..... it died. It was never there in the first place."

Poor woman, I feel worse for her than I feel for myself. She was mortified. I swear if I ever, ever, get pregnant again, I won't tell a soul until I'm literally ready to pop.

We brave Midnight Mass, especially since I'm helping out afterwards with the collection. Of course the vicar's sermon is about the Christmas baby and I feel the tears welling up in my eyes. I feel so terribly vulnerable in church. It's the one place where I feel there is no demand on me to be braver than I am. But that bloody collection afterwards ...

I try not to listen, why do I have to take it all so personally anyway? Surely the Christ child can hardly be compared to the pregnancy I've just lost. Vaguely I hear him say something about not everybody necessarily being happy at Christmas. Hello, what's that, some understanding in the sea of festive jollity? He goes on to talk about the cross of Easter already looming over the crib and speaks of the great tragedy inherent in the Christmas story. The Nativity is more than just a pretty tale about a baby in a crib. It's about life, about joy as well as pain and suffering, and shining through it all, the love and the mercy of God. Thank you Geoffrey! A sermon *'a la carte'*. It sometimes happens, and I'm grateful, even though I'm not talking to God right now. I'm as confused about God as I am about everything else. Still, the words give me comfort.

We bow our heads for a few moments of silence and then the servers begin the mammoth task of collecting the bumper harvest from the great masses that have come to hear the Christmas Gospel preached on this cold London night.

Outside church the homeless roam, for one night disturbed from their regular spots in the pews. For the troops, as they are affectionately called by the congregation, it will be warm soup and perhaps a bed for the night this Christmas Eve. And as the Christmas Spirit wanes into New Year's ennui, they will be forgotten again, except by those who spend their every day working with the very people who most resemble the homeless Christ child this night. The world's a funny place.

"Aunt Trudy has called to invite us down to Dartmouth for the New Year's weekend, it might be just what we need." Or just what I need, I think to myself. Peter is in the shower and makes half-hearted noises of interest.

"Apparently they have a great time there on New Year's Eve, dressing up and having a pub crawl from one end of the High Street to the other. It sounds just the thing." Taking encouragement from the silence that ensues from the bathroom I rattle on. "It would be something to look forward to and I need something to get this black cloud lifted. Of course, Pamela will also be there, now four months pregnant and apparently blooming, but we've always been great friends, so I'm sure I'll cope. After all, I wish her all the best, don't I?"

On and on I rattle, knowing that Peter, who spends his working day in constant social interaction has rather split feelings about private socialising. "The thing is, and we don't have to if we don't want to, but, they all dress up."

Now Peter exits the shower, his face still covered in shaving cream and a look of complete dread on his face.

"No dressing up! I'll come down to Dartmouth, they're a nice bunch of people, but no dressing up."

And so we agree that we go as ourselves, but just in case he changes his mind, I go and get us some costumes from the local party shop. Peter won't have to make much of an effort dressed as a monk and I'll be a tarted up Elizabethan barmaid. My breasts appear not to have realised I'm not pregnant anymore as they're still a size larger than the already quite formidable normal. So tarted up barmaid it is.

The drive down to Dartmouth seems to take forever, and poor old Peter has to drive the whole stretch. I'm terrible at estimating distances and thought he was being a bit of a sissy when he said it was a long way to drive on his own.

Our car is a manual, and since I only ever managed to get a license for an automatic car I can't drive this one. After more than eighty lessons in a manual I decided I was too co-ordinationally challenged to manage gear shifting, choke pushing, steering and watching the traffic all at the same time. It just seemed to make sense to take the automatic test instead. It's never bothered me before, but in my current state of mind all my flaws turn into major failures. And so every time Peter sighs and asks me to check how much further it is, I take it as a frontal attack on my general state of incompetence.

Finally, after a long dark drive through narrow winding lanes, too narrow for comfort in places, we see the twinkling lights of Dartmouth harbour.

We're greeted warmly and the mulled wine flows generously. No one talks about the miscarriage, and for once, I'm relieved. Maybe I'm starting to put it behind me. Pamela has already gone up to bed, so I'm even spared that tricky first moment for now. Then we go up to our room. Up two flights of stairs, round a narrow passageway, and up a step. The sweetest little room you can imagine. Tudor beams, a bed with a pink candlewick bedspread, a view of the harbour, and there, pushed up against the foot of the bed...

Oh bloody hell!

I throw myself on the bed.

How can anyone have been so insensitive. There is a cradle at the foot of the bed. A bloody cradle. Well I might want to be putting things behind me, and have a good time, but how the hell am I supposed to do that when I have a bloody empty cradle at my feet all night. Peter tries to move it into a corner, but there is no way to move the damn thing, perhaps the very reason why the cradle was there in the first place. It would have taken some serious manoeuvring to get it out of the room and down the hall. I rant and rave at the stupidity of people, but really, I'm ranting and raving at my own tremendous vulnerability, the ease with which my feelings are churned up, at the merest hint of anything baby.

Will this ever go away?

The next day at breakfast we plan ahead for the day. Pamela comes down and really does look quite wonderful. We sort of give each other a hug, and she suggests we all go off for a walk along the beach. I don't really feel much like spending any more time than I have to with someone who is so clearly and so successfully pregnant. But Peter and Ashton, Pam's husband, are already deep in conversation as they pull on their wellies, and I can't just go around being selfish all the time. It's not as if Pamela is flaunting it either, she hardly mentions the subject, only to say how sorry she is for us, and how hard she imagines it must be for me to be around pregnant women.

"It's different with you," I lie, "and it's not as if I feel a complete jealous wreck all of the time, (just most of the time ...). I feel really happy for you, and I hope all goes well."

Liar!

In the back of my head I've rehearsed words of comfort should something go wrong for them too. Well, at least it would make me feel needed again, rather than so terribly redundant and in need of help myself. I'm becoming such a bitch.

I change the subject.

"So tell me about work, are you going to go back after the birth?"

Pamela picks up the hint and starts to regale us with hilarious stories of mad colleagues and outrageous bosses. By the end of the walk it doesn't feel as if she is as pregnant anymore. It's more 'good old Pamela' who happens to be pregnant and I'm glad I made myself go with them after all.

In the evening Peter and I get pretty drunk. I feel a little smug towards poor Pamela who is deprived both of fags and booze. Peter is finally bullied into wearing his monk's garb, neither of us realising that with Pam dressed up as a nun it appears to be the height of fun to keep asking 'the monk' if he got 'the nun' pregnant. Oh what fun we're all having ....NOT.

Still, we get through the evening well enough, and as we raise our glasses to 1992 I promise myself that the coming year is going to be positive and good, and in the back of my mind a little voice says; *and maybe fruitful...*

Empty

I feel barren, hollow,
my belly an empty vessel under a broken heart.
Where once was life,
cries a soul torn apart.

My hand rests there,
where you should have been,
and I silently stifle
an anguished scream.

I see Mother Nature
rejuvenate once more
with the sickening ease
of a talented whore.

Who is to say, why me,
why not me.
If only I knew,
what the future would be.

Chapter 4

THE BIG DIP

As I return the costumes to the shop a week later, I notice I'm still feeling cross about the jokes people were making about the monk and the nun. If anyone is going to get pregnant by Peter it's me, and the sooner the better. Okay, so we haven't quite agreed yet on when to start trying again. Peter wants to wait until after the summer and I would rather try again as soon as possible. At the hospital they said three months, meaning we could give it a go again in February or March. Peter will be gone most of April, leaving May and then June, the month I would have given birth and I can't bear to think about how I'll be feeling then.

Perhaps Peter is right, deal with this first and then try coping with another pregnancy later. On the other hand, being pregnant might make things easier in terms of dealing with friends' pregnancies since Pamela is not the only one expecting a baby.

In the last months I've had to smile my way through the news that two of my closest friends have first babies on the way, as well as my sister-in-law. Thank goodness they are all abroad, so I won't have to be confronted with their bulging bellies. It just seems so terribly unfair. I had thought long and hard about starting a family, planned it all, stopped smoking, drinking, and yet it goes wrong. Yet none of them even seem to have thought it through, and one even called it a happy mistake.

"So why them and not me," I ask Peter, after a rather trying conversation with one friend who just won't realise that I'm not interested in hearing all about her morning sickness and her dizzy spells.

"Would it make you happier if your friends also had miscarriages?" he replies, playing devil's advocate.

"Of course not, it's the last thing I would wish upon anybody." That, at least, is the politically correct answer. Deep, deep down inside me the little voice says, *at least then someone would understand how I feel.*

"Perhaps you should try to keep your own feelings separate from what's going on in other people's lives. Try not to relate everything to yourself."

"And how the hell am I supposed to do that when friends seem intent on rubbing my nose into every single detail of their pregnancy."

"Is that really what they're doing?"

Well no, it's not what they're doing, but Peter has made a very perceptive remark and instead of letting his words reach my heart, I become defensive. "Do you think I enjoy being like this? I hate myself. I'm bitchy, jealous, petulant, and I really hate, hate pregnant women!"

Big cry ...

What's happening to me?

"You just need some time. Time to get over this. Instead of trying for another baby we should have a break and maybe go away somewhere really nice for your birthday." He puts his arms around me and with a sigh I lean my head against his shoulder.

Somewhere really nice, somewhere baby and belly-free. A pregnancy free zone!

A holiday wouldn't get me away from myself, but he means well, and I should at least count my blessings. I should count myself lucky to have Peter who, despite a Nordic inbred emotional inarticulateness, really, really tries. In fact, he is quite wonderful.

I'm the problem here. I don't know who I am or where I belong anymore. I'm not allowed to be part of that exclusive club of mothers and mothers-to-be and yet I've crossed the great divide between the women who are not even thinking of babies yet, and the women who are either in the process of becoming mothers, or have already succeeded. I'm in some kind of no-woman's land. I can't go back to a non-maternal state, and yet for some reason can't join that exclusive sorority of mothers either.

The confusion pervades everything I do. My work, my friendships, my relationship with Peter. This sense of not quite being a woman, not being able to fulfil this simple act of staying pregnant and having a baby. For thousands of years women have been fruitful and multiplied, but not me.

What an idiot. What a failure.

Can't drive a manual car, can't have babies.

It's house hunting time. We've been spending every spare moment in Hillingdon looking for a place to rent. Since we are one of the millions caught in the negative equity trap we have to resort to renting instead of buying. Our old flat will be rented out to Islington Council so that we can make the mortgage repayments as well as pay rent. It's a creative way out of a boring situation, and Peter compliments me on my inventiveness. True Lysanne. I suppose I still have my moments.

We finally decide on 'Badger House', a sweet whitewashed little detached house in a residential area. Having been townies for the past five years, we adjust very differently to suburban life. I enjoy it. Memories of the small village in Holland where I spent a large chunk of my growing years flood back. Everyone knowing everyone. A sense of belonging. A local church where you can get involved. It's a shame about St. Martin's and it's not as if I can't drive there in twenty minutes on a Sunday morning, but I feel I'm drifting away from them a little. I was quite disappointed that, having been part of a parish that is dedicated to looking after other people, I felt so little 'looked after' myself when I needed it.

I'm forgetting about Simon's words, about the Christmas sermon, and thinking about 'life back to normal' for the rest of the parish, when I still feel bruised and hurt. Maybe my switch of allegiance from St. Martin's in town to St. Jerome's here in Hillingdon has more to do with my own high expectations than reality, but still, that's how it is.

Peter and suburbia, on the other hand, do not mix. He is having a real attack of 'burb paranoia', and after a long rant and rave about being boring and middle of the road, he tells me he refuses to wash the car on Saturdays! Fine by me, not that he ever did ...

It's so exciting to have a house, with a proper garden, a garden gate and a garden path leading to a front door. It's a luxury you can't imagine unless you've lived three floors up on a busy road in North London. All those heavy shopping bags that don't need to be lugged up three flights of stairs anymore. And of course.... well, we won't think of that right now.

There was a bit of an embarrassed silence when the landlords mentioned we could turn one of the rooms into a nursery, the subject of babies not having cropped up in the conversation earlier. I bluntly tell it how it is, which was perhaps too blunt, judging by Peter's cringing look.

"We hardly know these people."

"Which is why they shouldn't assume we want to convert the room into a nursery. Maybe we don't even want babies. People shouldn't assume ..."

We've now had this conversation a million times, and Peter is just too fed up to engage in it anymore. But in his eyes I see what he thinks; perhaps you are also assuming a little too much yourself, Lysanne.

Our first guest is Mamma who traditionally comes to stay when Peter is off doing his three week Ice Hockey production. I proudly show her around Badger House, my first real house. We sit outside in the garden and have our breakfast in the little conservatory. We talk and talk, and have a lovely girlie time together. We shop at M&S, Boots and W.H. Smith, and visit all the other old haunts mamma remembers from the days our family used to live in England.

Finally, on her last day, I take her out for a drive in the country. We visit Cliveden House, have tea in the teddy bear's restaurant in Henley and lose our way as we drive home. As we pass through a tiny hamlet with a beautiful old church and a wonderfully preserved cloister garden we stop the car and have a wander around. It's so serene, so peaceful. I sense tranquillity and harmony and for the first time since the miscarriage, I think I can perhaps start to accept it and let it go.

Filled with serenity we get back into the car and decide that perhaps we were meant to lose our way, just as sometimes we lose our way in life, only to be presented with an unexpected gift. Over the past week we talked a lot about not getting what you want, when you want it, and about keeping your eyes open to receive the unexpected, rather than staring yourself blind on what you can't get. This detour seems to be the embodiment of that thought, and we sit in silent contemplation all the way home.

In many ways time is starting to heal my wounds. The new house, a new car, this time automatic, my mother's visit, a conference in Nice, a visit from friends in Holland and my birthday, it all helps. I also don't feel the need to talk about the miscarriage all the time anymore. In fact, I'm getting rather bored of hearing myself going on about it.

I feel ready to start trying for another baby, but I can't raise the subject with Peter since he is away for most of this month. When I do think about becoming pregnant again, I automatically think about how or when it might go wrong. The two thoughts just seem automatically linked together. I notice that I've become more pessimistic than I used to be and I suppose I see Life in a less naive light. Shit just happens and you have to accept it with Grace. Well, that's the theory, although I don't really live it out other than in rare moments such as when mamma and I found the cloister garden. I can't say I like this new realistic me, but certainly the innocence is gone. The blind trust with which I've let Life, God, take me forward, is tarnished. I don't want to be held by the hand anymore. I'll plan my own route, and play things my own way from now on.

In a rare moment of synchronicity Georgy asks me how my faith has been affected by the miscarriage. It's something my mother and I also talked about when she was here. All my friends know that, although not a bible basher or religious freak, my faith means a lot to me. I made them sit through an entire Anglican wedding service, though we spared them Communion. For a lot of friends this was the first meaningful service they had been to in many years, and they were surprised at the lightness and the jollity of it, not in the least caused by a tri-lingual liturgy.

"So how does your God figure in all of this?" It's not meant as an attack, quite the opposite, Georgy is concerned about the major quarrel that is going on between 'Him up there' and me.

"I don't know," I answer cagily, "I guess I'm a bit pissed off. There I am, lighting candles, giving thanks, being a good girl, stopping smoking, blah, blah, and what does He do, He makes me a baby and then takes it away again. God as the ultimate mover and shaker. God whose hand steered me towards England, towards Peter, and now, towards this complete and utter non-event. How could He let me down like this?"

Georgy sits quietly as she listens to my angry ranting. Casts a few anxious glances heavenward as my tirade becomes rather too personally abusive to God, and then, being Georgy, calmly bursts my angry bubble with the following observation.

"Darling. I understand you feel let down, but I think you are being terribly unfair to your God. You sound like someone who has always had excellent service from the same shop. Nice people, good products, the odd bargain. And now, just the once, you've been sold something with a manufacturing error, and their entire reputation and all the goodwill built up over the years is gone in one fell swoop. Perhaps they are trying..... perhaps your God is trying, to make up for it, but you're just too bloody angry to listen."

Ouch! And spot on. Food for thought.

Back home, and still thinking about what Georgy has said, I sit down and write a letter to God. Writing is, after all, the way I express myself best, and anything I pray right now just goes right out the window. My image of a Sunday school God who makes everything work out is shattered.

As I write, a new image comes to me, that of a parent. The very thing I've just failed to become. Yet a good parent can let her children go, despite knowing that life will knock them about and give them a hard time. A good parent knows she can't protect her child from these things, not if they are to grow up free and strong. Yet a good parent is also there to run to for comfort.

As I write my image of God changes, as I begin to understand Him as a Divine Parent, who allows us to run to Him for comfort whenever we fall over and tear open our knees on life's rough gravel, but who lets us loose in life to make our own mistakes and get hurt. I realise something else. Don't expect Him to remove the gravel for you. Why should He, remove it for you, and not for anyone else.

Writing the letter is a humbling and yet illuminating experience. I feel a great calm descending. Now perhaps I can really start to pick up the pieces.

One moment I'm serene and accepting, and then I go right back down again. As June approaches I feel myself slowly sinking down into an immeasurably deep pool of sadness and despair. The worst thing is, no one seems to notice, not even Peter. To the outside world I'm the happy cheerful person they want me to be. Strong, coping, getting over it. Yet I wake up every morning knowing that a part of me is forever gone. I still feel the emptiness in my belly, the ache in my heart. I imagine holding my baby, cradling it against my breast, feeding it, loving it. One more week, and the baby would have been born. Perhaps it might have already been born. A boy or a girl?

"Try to stop thinking so much about it," they say, I just wish I could. I wish I could become the person I was, genuinely happy, not filled with anger and hatred against the world and especially against myself. I say to Peter that the coming week might be tough. He is in the middle of doing something else and doesn't really take in what I say.

"Why?" he asks.

I stalk out of the room, I slam the door, no baby to wake up.

I light up a cigarette. Why the hell not. My body punished me, I'll punish it back. I've put on a stone. At least if I can't be pregnant I might still look pregnant. What's the point of trying to lose it anyway, if I'm going to blow up like a balloon the next time round. When ..... if ...

We're watching a film. Man – woman – meet – marry – have baby. I switch over to another channel. Peter is getting used to this. Last month I threw the remote control at the television after one too many happy nappy ads. It cost us £20 to get a new remote control. It will cost a lot more to get me back on my feet.

Buried under a pile of papers is the leaflet I was given at the hospital. The leaflet with advice, help lines, contact persons. It's a small beacon sending out signals. I don't want to ask for help, I don't need help, I've never needed help. Shit, I've never needed help more than I need it now. Bleep, bleep, the beacon sends out its signals, I ignore it. I dread the phone ringing, news of Pamela's baby, the Dutch friends' babies. I cancel all appointments, then I take the day off, and another, and another. Peter calls Georgy and asks her to come round. He is at a loss – whatever he says is wrong, whatever he does is wrong, and as for a sex life, well, that's for other people. Yet he sticks by me, he's very loyal but I'm also making his life a misery. Even mamma is starting to despair of me. I tried the tough act, failed, had a moment of serenity and insight, lost it, and now she feels I'm wallowing in my sorrows. I wish. At least wallowing has some aura of enjoyment about it, this is not fun, this is hell.

Georgy comes over and helps me look for the papers from the hospital. Bleep, bleep goes the beacon, I know exactly where they are. Georgy argues that it's a sign of strength to ask for help, not weakness. Admitting you have a problem is half the problem solved. I think of the magazines I got from the Miscarriage Association, just after it happened. They just made me feel worse. Georgy says that perhaps I wasn't ready for it then, or perhaps it wasn't the right thing. Don't close off all avenues, just because one didn't work.

She leaves me sitting by the phone with the papers on my lap. Standing by the door her last words to me are: "It's up to you now, but remember, we're right behind you."

I sit and stare at the wall for ages, then I call the number on the paper. I ask for Miriam. The receptionist asks if I want to leave a message. What the hell am I supposed to say: "Tell her I've had a miscarriage and still can't get over it six months later?" I feel such a fool. She must have sensed my hesitation and asks if it's about a miscarriage. Apparently that is Miriam's main area of work. I sort of mumble that it is, but immediately add that I'm not sure if going to a group is necessarily what I need. She suggests sending out some additional material that I'll have in the post tomorrow, and in the meantime she will leave a message for Miriam to call me later today. Half an hour later the phone rings and I stare at it for a full thirty seconds before I pick up.

"Hello, Lysanne speaking."

"Hello, it's Miriam, from the Health Centre," and then very quietly, compassionately, "I'm so sorry to hear of your loss."

I just burst into tears and sob.

I'm so sorry to hear that you have lost your baby. Finally someone putting words to how I feel, someone who acknowledges without a word of explanation how much it hurts, how big this is for me, how devastating. Miriam waits patiently on the other end of the phone until I stop sobbing.

"Do you think I could maybe come round tomorrow afternoon, I have to be in your area anyway, would that suit you?"

No pressure, not making me feel like I've actually asked for any help, just responding to the great need I'm communicating to talk to someone about this. We agree that she will come round tomorrow at three. I promise to have tea and biscuits ready. Miriam admonishes me just to think of myself.

A summer storm has been brewing outside all day. It matches my inner mood, dark clouds with odd bursts of blue sky and bright sunshine. Just making the call yesterday has brought great peace. My lingering sadness has been validated, it's acceptable to feel the way I feel.

As three o'clock approaches I get butterflies in my tummy, I'm nervous about the visit. Is this where they decide I've gone completely loony and need to spend some time on a funny farm? What if Miriam was just masking a great concern for my wellbeing, thinking I was on the verge of going nuts. What if..... but then the doorbell rings.

Miriam is dressed in her health visitor's uniform, and looks tremendously reassuring. She's from 'up North' which means that every word she utters has the round soothing overtones of the Yorkshire Dales. I immediately feel at ease with her. We decide to sit in the conservatory and make small talk as I prepare some tea and put biscuits on a plate. I tell her about Holland and having a Swedish husband, she talks about being from Yorkshire.

Just as we sit down the storm breaks with intense ferocity. Raindrops lash the roof of the conservatory, turning into hailstones that threaten to smash their way through the glass. We can't make ourselves heard above the clamour of the storm. Flashes of lightning are immediately followed by rolling thunderclaps. No time to count the seconds between lightning and thunder, it's right overhead. We just look at each other and smile. We don't go inside, because there is something magic and cleansing about this hellish weather breaking above our heads. I experience the storm as a tremendous release, something lifts itself up and out of me, I suddenly feel freer, lighter, and I wonder what Miriam and I will talk about once the storm abates.

Then it's over. The clouds move away as quickly as they came. Miriam asks me if I still want to talk about the miscarriage. I'm glad she asks, because I realise I do.

"How far gone were you in your pregnancy when you lost the baby?"

"I was pregnant for thirteen weeks, but I actually never lost the baby, it was never there to begin with."

"But you didn't know that, for thirteen weeks you thought you were going to have a baby."

She's put her finger on it. "Yes, and now I feel a real idiot for thinking that it was true. I feel really tricked."

"And sad......?" she asks with her head cocked to one side.

"I just can't shake it off, however hard I try. Sometimes it drives me mad."

"Perhaps you are trying too hard, perhaps you need to ease up on yourself a bit and accept that you've really been dealt a nasty blow."

"If other people didn't make that so hard...," I retort angrily. "People say such stupid things, like telling me I'm young enough to have another one." Miriam pulls a face, she's heard that one before. "And telling me that it's really common. I feel like telling them that old people dying is really common too, but you don't go and tell that to the widow do you?"

Miriam laughs at the absurdity of it, but at the same time she remains sympathetic, and certainly doesn't tell me to stop saying such horrible things. Instead, she hears me out, and then complements what I've told her with examples of other women's experiences. What a relief, just to know that other women have felt the same way, not only about their pregnancies, but also about the way people respond, about other pregnant women, about their partners. It's tremendously reassuring to know that I'm not going mad.

"And then there's my cousin Pamela, whose baby is due any day. We should have been enjoying our pregnancies together, but now ... I feel so cut off." I tell her how hard I find it to talk to her, in fact, the last months I haven't talked to her at all. I just talk to her mum, Trudy, but I can't really bear to hear her telling me about the impending birth, even though I know that for my aunt having children wasn't exactly without traumas either.

"I try to be generous, I try to listen and say nice things, but it hurts so much inside. And I know I have to go and see the new baby when it's born, but I'm so scared of the feelings it will arouse in me. Not that I would hurt the baby, but I'm jealous, so terribly jealous." I hardly dare look at Miriam, she must think I'm being a real bitch. But when I do look into her face all I see is compassion.

"Stop judging yourself so hard. It's normal to feel like you do, and I actually think you've been asking more of yourself than you need to."

I tell her about the discussion I had with Peter, about wishing miscarriages upon my dearest friends, well, not really wishing it upon them, but wishing there was someone who shared my experience.

"There was an interview on Oprah the other day, with the male lead from 'Dirty Dancing'. I can't think of his name right now. Anyway, someone in the audience asked when he and his wife were going to start a family. He skirted around the issue a bit, and didn't give a straight answer. Then the pushy audience member asked again, and he told her that the subject was actually quite painful because they had just suffered a miscarriage. You could hear the embarrassment oozing out of the box. But I was delighted, here's someone who is on my team. I even wanted to write him and his wife a letter..... that shows how far gone I am!" I conclude, once more daring her to tell me that yes, I really had gone over the top.

Miriam does no such thing, she listens, she nods, and she doesn't try to tell me to feel any different than I feel. Doesn't try to persuade me to behave like a better person, just listens and listens, until I feel heard. Finally, when I can't think of anything else I want to talk about, she hands me an invitation to a monthly meeting of women who have suffered miscarriages. A support group. As she leaves she winks and says, "we actually have quite a lot of fun too you know, so don't feel put off by the idea that we all sit and despair together, we share each other's tears as well as laughter."

And with that, she's out of the door.

I heave an immense sigh of relief. I'm not going mad, there are other women out there who feel the same. I shoot a little prayer up to heaven to thank God for people like Miriam, and when I clear away the teacups, I find myself singing out loud for the first time in months. My talk with Miriam has really helped, and I'm wondering if I even need to go to the support group. Perhaps it was enough for me that she acknowledged my feelings and helped me to understand that there are other women who feel exactly the same as I do.

A few days later the phone goes, it's mamma. "Pam had a little boy, Lysanne," mamma's voice is soft and reaches out to me. "It was a very difficult birth and they are still in the hospital, but they're fine."

What can I say. I know I need to be told, but I don't want to hear a single word more. A baby boy for Pamela, that's what I would have wanted, three little boys, that was my wish. Now I daren't wish for anything anymore.

"Are you alright?"

No I'm bloody well not, my whole day is messed up and I just want someone to hold me and care about me. It hurts so much. I can't buy a card, Peter will have to do it. I feel guilty again but then I remember what Miriam said; don't be too hard on yourself. Pam will be busy getting used to her new life as a mum, and she won't miss me coming round. Peter says he is sure she'll understand, but a part of me feels a bit of a misery guts to cop out like this. Duty calls and all that! Peter calls and makes a date for us to come round after we have returned from holiday. That's fine by them, and also by me.

Peter is relieved the talk with Miriam has done me so much good and is now looking forward even more to the three weeks we'll be spending in Sweden during the summer break. I'm looking forward to just taking it easy and enjoying each other's company. There will be a big party in Karlstad for my father-in-law who is turning 75, and then Peter and I will motor up to the north of Sweden in a borrowed car to spend some time at his mum's summer house in Norrtälje, right on the Baltic sea.

It's paradise, just like the rest of Sweden. It's so out of the way and deserted that you can walk around in your birthday suit all day and no one would notice. The perfect place to try to pull myself together a bit more, and build up strength, emotional strength, for another attempt. On this Peter and I have agreed. We might even try to make a Norrtälje baby. My sister-in-law is heavily pregnant and will be about to drop when we come over. I hope I'll be fine with that. At least I'll have the knowledge that we're back in the game, and that helps.

After a typical Swedish summer party, with lots of 'skolling' and speeches, we reach the little summer house on the Baltic. It is a tiny old fashioned Swedish cottage, built by Peter's grandfather, with neither running water nor electricity. The toilet is a couple of yards behind the house, and you need to have a strong stomach and be in great need in order to visit it. We haul water from a well and carry it in a bucket up to the house. It's amazing how environmentally friendly your water usage suddenly becomes when you're hauling it up yourself.

The fridge is no more than a larder, a cavern cut into the rock with a large wooden door in front. Peter has been well trained by his mother not to trust any food that has been out of this 'cooler' for more than an hour, and diligently puts things back into the larder as soon as we have eaten our breakfast, lunch or dinner. From the little veranda you look out over the water, with boats sailing by in the sunshine, and occasionally a large ferry boat on its way out to Finland.

We read all day, play cards all night, and sleep till late into the morning. We're in a perfect rhythm. Up at eleven, to bed at two. And being this far north, it hardly gets dark. The magic of sitting outside at one o'clock in the morning and still being able to read the book that you are holding on your lap. Seeing the sky turn a wonderful shade of orange and red as the sun dips down under the horizon and almost immediately comes up over it again. Watching the glowing colours of the sunset become all at once the glowing colours of dawn.

A new dawn.

Our new dawn!

Of course, we haven't forgotten about making a Norrtälje baby either, but there's no pressure. We practise a lot, and getting pregnant will happen when it happens, although it doesn't stop me working out when the baby, if any, would arrive ... Will I ever learn?

We're home. No Norrtälje baby. My period just arrived heralded by two hours of stomach cramps. I really must do something about that. I'm quite okay about not being pregnant. Even a little relieved. Part of me is terribly scared to be pregnant again, or rather, to miscarry again. We'll just have to keep on having fun trying.

I was sent a letter from the miscarriage group while I was away in Sweden, inviting me to come to one of their evenings. I wonder if I should still go now that we're trying for another baby. Perhaps it won't do me much good to listen to women talking about miscarriages. After all, I need to try to be in an as positive mind as possible. I also don't know if I really dare to sit and share my sorrows with a whole group of strangers. On the other hand, I complain about people not paying any attention to what has happened, and perhaps this way, I can have a place where I can focus on my feelings, while getting on with my normal life the rest of the time. I'm still not quite sure, we'll see.

I've just had the strangest experience. I was out walking on Hampstead Heath when I was suddenly hit with this overwhelming sense of knowing that we will have one more small mishap, and then everything will be okay. What on earth is that supposed to mean? I'm not even pregnant again, am I?

Mamma sometimes calls me her white witch, and is convinced I have psychic powers, but this is silly. Still, it leaves me feeling even more uncomfortable about trying for another baby, or maybe not. Part of the problem is that you don't know what to expect. If someone said to me, "I'm very sorry, you are going to have three more miscarriages and then ten healthy children," I think I could cope. It's not knowing that makes it so hard. At least for me, woman of little trust.

We're on our way to see Pamela's baby. Peter keeps looking sideways at me in the car and asking; "you okay?" He knows how much I dread this visit. Her baby might have been my baby. Her baby would have been a playmate for my baby. Her baby was somehow linked to my baby, but mine never happened and hers did. Yet I feel the time is right to go and say hello.

Peter and I make a deal. If I say that I'm getting cold, it's a sign for Peter to start making our goodbye's. We also have another date to go on to afterwards, so they know we won't be staying long. They're not stupid either, they know this is tough on us, and in that way, also for them. How on earth are they supposed to react? They shouldn't be feeling guilty about having a healthy baby, should they?

As we're about to drive up to the house I realise we still don't have a present. Back to the High Street and to Boots. I buy a really lovely basket with lots of pampering soaps and lotions for Pamela. The birth was absolutely awful, and I feel really sorry for her that she is still in so much pain, although part of me can't help thinking that she should feel thankful for having been giving birth at all. No present for little Toby though. Sorry baby, I'll make it up to you one day. I'm just not up to browsing through baby wear yet.

Their little baby boy is asleep upstairs when we come. For a moment it's just like a year ago. Two young couples, our marriages only a few months apart, having a drink and a snack in the garden. Then, even before Pam does, I hear the baby crying. I brace myself and then .... the strangest thing happens. I feel a tremendous sense of joy. The primitive joy and amazement at the miracle of new life. Why on earth was I scared to be upset by this tiny little person. He's gorgeous, scrawny, ugly and beautiful at the same time, as only fresh from the press babies can be. I'm not too interested in all the stories about how he eats or sleeps, but I don't mind holding this little bundle, just for a little while anyway.

I feel Peter's eyes on me, am I cold he asks me. I smile up at him, no not cold, a little emotional, but not cold. The tears come later, as they always do, and I lie awake thinking about holding little Toby. It felt so normal and so right to be holding something so tiny and warm. I still get annoyed at television programmes where the honeymoon scene is almost immediately followed by the scene of a heavily pregnant new wife being rushed to the hospital delivery room, but actual real babies, no. I realise they don't hurt me at all.

Tonight the miscarriage support group is meeting. All day I hover between copping out, and reminding myself how good it felt to talk to Miriam. I also think about the fact that this time last year I was just pregnant. Right up until the last minute I dither, then, with a final shove towards the door, Peter says, "go on, and if it's awful you just come right back. What have you got to lose?"

I find the building easily and so arrive at least ten minutes early. Miriam is standing by the door greeting people. Her beaming face reassures me.

"Lysanne, you made it."

I'm well impressed. With a name like Lysanne, you get used to people calling you all kinds of things, from Lasagne to Lausanne. I try to explain why three meetings have come and gone before I turn up, but she seems quite used to this kind of erratic behaviour. "You took a big step coming here," she says, "I hope you'll feel it was the right thing to do." And with that, she leads me into a room and gestures around the chairs that have been arranged in a circle in the middle of the room. Two chairs are already occupied, and I go and sit next to a slim woman who looks my own age. Her name is Anne, and she has been coming to the group for over six months.

"Oh, I'm not sure if I'll be coming quite such a long time."

Coward.

Anne was first told she was infertile, then had an ectopic pregnancy, and is now having tests to find out if she could become pregnant again. Later I realise that they are all extremely familiar with the medical jargon, and trade their experiences of the tests and investigations that are available. Then I remember Miriam telling me that they quite often invite guest speakers from Hillingdon Hospital, so it's a forum for sharing information, as well as feelings. While we sit and talk another woman walks into the room. She is greeted with a lot of warmth and enthusiasm by the rest. It appears that last time she was here she had told them she was expecting. After the initial enthusiastic greeting, they all somehow tap into the fact that she is not responding in the same manner.

"What happened?" someone asks.

"I lost it in the eighteenth week."

"How many does that make now?"

"Four."

I feel a lump starting in my throat and I turn to her as she comes and sits down on the other side of me. I want to say something really helpful, really comforting, but what can you say to someone who has had four miscarriages? I just stare and look stupid. Then it hits me out of the blue, this is maybe how other people have felt around me. I sit quietly and digest that insight.

"Any chance they will start investigating now?"

And a conversation follows about all the different tests that are possible and how awful it is that they don't start trying to find out the cause of recurrent miscarriages until you have had at least three. However, most of the conversation goes over my head. Four miscarriages, and I'm sitting here feeling miserable and pitiful because I have had one. I feel like sinking into the floor. How on earth has this bubbly, warm person sitting next to me survived four miscarriages.

The meeting is called to order and we have a chance to introduce ourselves. It turns out this group, this particular constellation of women, have been coming for the past couple of months. As they each, briefly, tell their story I feel more and more of a fraud. Ten years of infertility, then pregnant, then a miscarriage, four miscarriages, someone with an ectopic pregnancy, where the baby grows in the fallopian tube... When my turn comes I come out with it at once.

"Uh, well, listening to you all, I feel I'm being a bit of a baby here." Oops, bad choice of words. "I've only had the one miscarriage, and I've been really down. I'm amazed listening to you all, how you seem to cope so well."

The response is overwhelming.

"One miscarriage is already more than enough to feel bad about, and no, we're not coping all of the time. The group is what helps us cope, and we actually end up having a lot of fun too."

What a wonderful bunch of people. I listen to their stories as they talk about best friends having babies, mothers-in-law making them feel bad for not producing a grandchild, you're young, you'll have another type comments, about wanting to kick the pregnant woman at the counter at Sainsbury's who already has a gaggle of unruly kids trailing behind her. And then the laughter, amid the tears, the sense of community, the sense that finally, at last, here is a group of women I can identify with, a whole group of women in this no-woman's land of 'non-mothers', inexplicably excluded from the club.

I'm on a high when I come home. It's done me the world of good! I'm determined to go again, unless of course, I fall pregnant, and then we'll wait and see.

Friendship

From such small things a friendship grows,
a gentle word, someone who knows,
a wink, a smile, a passing glance,
a spontaneous gesture,
an open stance.

On such small things a friendship builds,
more gentle words, and to be still,
sharing of thoughts, a gentle nudge,
bridges to build,
bridges of love.

More precious than pearls,
more splendid than gold,
is a friendship that is valued,
and of its value is told.

Chapter 5

NOT AGAIN

And then we'll wait and see...... famous last words. Last week I was pregnant. This week I'm not. Baby been and gone, all in the space of eight days.

I was thinking back to that weird premonition I had on Hampstead Heath. Well, if that's true, it means that the sooner I get it over and done with, the sooner we'll be on to winning pregnancy number three. I feel really weird. Not sad, certainly not happy. A bit bamboozled I suppose. The whole thing was over in record time. I missed my period on the Monday, went to see Dr. Walker on the Wednesday, had it confirmed on the Friday and started bleeding that same night.

Thankfully, a week is not really enough to allow yourself to get excited about being pregnant, especially with the mountain of reserve we built up following last year's episode. At least it seems I won't have to go into hospital this time round. I count my blessings.

I've rested a bit during the weekend, and now I'm back at the office as if nothing has happened, just a late period. The phone goes, it's mamma. I've been on her mind all weekend, she says, and she just wants to know if I'm okay? Typical mamma. It makes me feel loved and cared about, and softens me. I end up sobbing down the phone as I tell her what happened in the past week. Okay, it does hurt. If nothing else, the unfairness of it all. Why the hell should I get pregnant only to lose it again. Mamma makes comforting noises, but I can hear in her voice that she too is sad for us. What can she do? What can anyone do?

When we hang up I set the office phone to voicemail and walk straight out towards the canal, tears streaming down my face. After Peter and I moved out to West London I persuaded my bosses in Washington that it would also be an excellent location for our offices. Cheaper than central London, close to Heathrow, and, although not on the list of arguments I presented to them, within cycling distance of my new home. An example of how I used to be able to set things to my hand, fix things, organise things so that they worked for me.

Part of the tears streaming down my face are tears of frustration. I can't fix this, I can't send off a couple of faxes and use my inexhaustible energy and charm to get what I want. That hurts, as much as anything else. Now I've also missed the latest meeting of the support group. I didn't attend because I suspected I was pregnant and told myself it would be indelicate to go.... well, I'm not known for my discretion and would have wanted to tell them about it. Or is that an excuse? Perhaps I didn't really want to hear stories of pregnancies going wrong, didn't want to be around 'unlucky' people.... Ouch, what a bitch. Serves me right that I now wish I'd been there.

Two weeks have gone by and I'm still bleeding. Peter wants me to go and see Dr. Walker again but I am sick of doctors and just hope it will go away. I do wonder what's going on though. It's bad enough having a normal period, let alone one that goes on for two weeks. I don't have any cramps, and thought I'd get away without them this time, courtesy of an early miscarriage. Now I'm not so sure.

Finally I pluck up my courage and make an appointment at the surgery. Dr. Walker suggests a trip to the hospital for a scan to make sure that there is nothing left in the womb. He talks about maybe having lost one of twins. So much for counting my blessings, and hoping I would not be going to hospital. No such luck.

This time I go to the maternity wing to be scanned. I had picked up from the group that this was the place to be scanned, even though it's tough to sit amongst all those successfully pregnant women. However, one of the founding members of the group, this amazing person called Tina, has managed to organise a half an hour for possible miscarriage cases, before the general maternity scans. I feel strangely pleased that at least this time round I know what's expected of me as I take another sip of my 2 litre can of water.

Hope is a funny thing, it never really dies, and despite all the signs to the contrary I quietly play with the thought that perhaps they will see this wonderfully brave little clump of cells battling away in there. Vain hope. All they see is an empty womb. On the advice of the doctor they decide to admit me for a D&C, just in case ... I get on the phone to Peter. I'm very businesslike. I organise for him to go and get some overnight stuff for me and meet me in casualty, where I have to wait for the triage nurse to see me. I read somewhere that too many D&C's can cause problems further down the line in a successful pregnancy, and wonder if it's really necessary.

Peter arrives about an hour later and we sit together in casualty, resigned to the events of the next 24 hours. It really does make a difference to know what I have lying ahead of me this time, and I feel a lot more confident. I'm taking it all rather in my stride, and efficiently inform the nursing staff of all they need to be informed of. I make the impression of someone who is incredibly in control of the situation and knows the routine.

Somewhere deep inside I know I'm being too calm, too coldly efficient, but I don't want anyone to burrow deeper into my feelings than I myself am prepared to do. So I lie low for now, literally.

Just before I go down to the operating room I tell anyone who wants to hear that I was in a lot of pain last time and that despite the fact that I'm no sissy, God forbid, I really want someone standing by with a heavy dose of something other than pethidine when I come round from the anaesthetic. Everyone promises to pass the information on to the nursing staff in the recovery room. And then, history repeats itself ... a needle in my hand, the voice of the anaesthetist counting backwards ... oblivion.

Pain, again!

Bloody hell. I'm in such pain. I shout and scream, despite being severely told off by the nurses. I don't care. I try to climb off my trolley. I'm going to make a bloody nuisance of myself until they give me something, anything, to stop the pain. I'm going to be a pain until they give me something for the pain. I refuse to be in pain as well as lose my pregnancy. It adds insult to injury. I make a fuss, no more good girl, pain in the bloody arse. The registrar is called and they hover just out of earshot casting rather irritated looks my way. One nurse even admonishes me that I'm not the only one there.

Tough!

I need attention!

Finally something is injected directly into the needle in my hand, and once again.... oblivion.

I come to on the ward, but I'm extremely groggy. It's late at night. Once again Caesareans and difficult births taking precedence over those of us failing to provide new life, and once again Peter is sitting next to the bed. He looks so sad, and very tired. I try to talk but I don't make any sense. Finally, he gives me a kiss on my forehead and tells me how much he loves me. I just nod, giggle and doze off again.

This time, coming back from the hospital and into the swing of things is easier than I thought it would be. I sort of feel annoyed and irritated with the whole thing, want to put it behind me and forget about it. Only our closest friends know what has happened, and those colleagues that need to know. Again I get flowers, both from my own and from Peter's colleagues. I can't help noticing that the bunches are getting smaller though. At this rate, we're going to cost them a small fortune. I certainly don't have that same urge to talk about it all the time like I had the first time round. A sort of miscarriage ennui has taken hold of me. At least I'll be physically back on my feet again in a few days.

No such luck! I'm still bleeding on and off. My back and shoulders are really sore, and I feel absolutely drained. I haven't been able to go back to work and I resent the fact that this miscarriage is turning into a medical drama. Why can't I just miscarry and be done with it, why do I feel like a pest to the entire medical world for coming back again and again telling them something is wrong.

I sit at home on the sofa and try to make sense of things. Who can I ask for help. I don't want to keep calling Dr. Walker's surgery, and when I called the Gynea Ward for advice they told me to give it a few more days. Mamma suggests I talk to my brother. He is, after all, a medical student, and might be able to throw some light on things. He calls me a little while later and we have a long chat. One thing sticks in my brain. We talk about this instinctive feeling of 'this is wrong'. Whatever symptoms a patient has, whatever their history, every human being has a 'this is wrong signal' somewhere, and if that starts flashing, both doctor and patient should take note.

I'm a relatively sane woman, I even tend to err on the side of caution rather than hysteria, but my 'this is wrong' signal is definitely starting to flash. My mind keeps going back to the girl in the group who had the ectopic pregnancy. I even asked the radiographer who did the scan whether the pregnancy might be ectopic. She said they would have seen, and not to worry. Anyway, who am I to start making diagnoses?

To cheer me up Georgy picks me up in the car to go to a posh auction. Priceless furniture and rugs that Peter and I could never afford in a lifetime. The fun is in watching others and pretending. I actually forget the drama's of the past weeks for a while and enjoy the bidding process, minks and Mercs present and correct. A different world, and certainly a world away from the threatening sight of mums in the park with their babies in prams.

Suddenly I feel this terrible urge to go to the loo. I just manage to make it to the cubicle when I fall on all fours, doubled up with cramp. Now what? My 'this is wrong' light now flashes bright red. This is either the worst case of gastroenteritic cramps, or there is something much, much worse going on. One moment savouring the pretence of hobnobbing with the snob brigade and the next on the floor, in a not so clean toilet, in excruciating pain. Despite the pain, my brain does overtime. Will Georgy get worried, will she come to look for me, what will I say? This is just too embarrassing. What if a stranger comes walking in. I struggle to my feet and edge back into the main auction room. I find a chair to sit on at the back as I catch my breath. Very slowly the pain eases off.

Once more I'm bleeding.

Georgy wants to take me straight round to the hospital, but I decline. "I'm much better now."

Coward!

I'm just too bloody scared. Too scared even to acknowledge my flashing red light. I make my way home and pray that this will not happen again. I promise to call Dr. Walker as soon as I get to a phone. Home again I manage to put the whole thing into perspective and pretend that it wasn't that bad after all. Probably was cramps, something I ate. I don't tell her about the blood.

Two days later it happens again, this time in the office. As I lie curled up in a ball on the floor under my desk I manage to jerk the phone down from the shelf and thankfully get hold of Peter at once. He only works a few blocks away and he jumps into the car and picks me up, half carrying me down the stairs into the car. I can now no longer stand or sit, I hang in the passenger seat next to him and all I can do is whimper. Peter is scared too, but he drives calmly to the hospital, demands immediate attention from the nurses and manages to get me taken straight into a cubicle. Do not pass triage, do not collect £200.

By now I don't care about the miscarriage anymore, I just want them to sort me out. Despite being almost unable to breathe from the pain I'm still trying to justify the fact that I'm turning up at this hospital two weeks after they told me I was fine. Thankfully Peter has none of these hang-ups, and starts to boss and order people about until we get seen.

The pain has eased off by the time a junior doctor comes in to see me. I do yet another pregnancy test, she takes my temperature, and examines me. She prods my tummy, and touches the tip of the cervix with her finger.

"Does this hurt?"

I know from the talk with my brother that this is one way of diagnosing an ectopic, but in my case it doesn't hurt at all. Again we go through the events of the past four weeks. She sends me for another scan and this time I'm wheeled there on a hospital trolley. I'm starting to feel like a piece of meat on a slab. Prodded and pushed, the real me disappears somewhere deep into myself. It's safer there. They scan me and decide to do yet another D&C, the second in two weeks, just to be on the safe side. Somebody suggests I might have picked up an infection during the last D&C or after it. My temperature is slightly raised. I'm beyond caring, I just let myself be pushed from one end of the hospital to the other, Peter trudging along behind. I start to feel so dirty, so undignified. Nothing is sacred anymore. I don't ever want to end up like this again.

On my way down to the operating room the porter recognises me and makes the terribly ill-placed joke about me liking it here so much I keep coming back for more. With my last spark of defiance I tell him to shut the hell up!! I dread coming round from the anaesthetic again. What will I have to do this time to get them to stop the pain? Dance the hula hula?

No hula, hula, they remembered me from last time.... but I still feel jolly uncomfortable. Soon the ward will be visited by the consultant's team and there is a quiet expectant hush in the room. I'm becoming an expert on hospital hierarchy and ranking. The young lady prodding and poking me down in casualty was the youngest and most inexperienced member of the gynaecology and obstetrics team. Then there is the junior registrar, who has actually made this her chosen field and who one can assume has already seen a thing or two. Then there is the senior registrar, and by now we are talking experience. This is someone who has probably well and truly earned their spurs, yet still does most of the 24 hours shifts, and is waiting for a good consultant's post to come up. Finally, there is the head honcho, so important that as a regular patient, you never get to see her. She is no longer referred to as Dr. but Ms., or in the case of a gentleman doctor, Mr.

Then there is the slang.... it's not the gynaecology and obstetrics registrar, no it's the gynea reg.

I'm quite proud of all this totally useless, and probably incorrect, knowledge. What is it about the human psyche that makes us patients want to be on the 'in' side of this medical drama? Does it make us feel a little more in control? A little more part of a world that actually no one in their sane mind would want to be a part of? I lie and ponder on this as I wait for the doctors to bring me their verdict.

I missed last night's meeting of the support group (again), but Peter has called and spoken to Miriam and she sends her warmest greetings. She has promised Peter to call on me once I'm out of hospital. She apparently has also been in touch with the ward, because the ward sister, June, comes and spends some time sitting on my bed and giving me a bit of special attention. She mentions that she too comes to the group from time to time and that perhaps we will see each other there one evening. I've only been there once, yet I feel their care and support actually reaching out to me here in the hospital.

I ask June how the group started, whether it was perhaps a hospital initiative. Apparently it was a patient, just like myself, who decided that the way women were being treated when they came in for miscarriages just wasn't adequate, at least not on an emotional level. I think of the hospital porter and I nod my head. I'm not one to hold grudges or to seek to place blame, but looking back over the past few weeks, I suppose I too would have liked for some things to have been different. This patient, Tina, had asked June to help her lobby for ways to make the system better, and to start a group that would support women once they were back home trying to cope with the emotional aftermath of their miscarriages. It's the same Tina who had managed to organise special scans for women with threatened miscarriages at the maternity department. I'm impressed, what a way to channel your disappointment.

A hush falls over the ward as the duty consultant's team appears. We obediently hop into our beds and await their verdict. In my case it's 'good news' and 'bad news', some more 'good news' and finally some devastating news. The first 'good' news is that apparently there is no sign of an infection or a pregnancy left in the womb. The scrapings, more jargon, only revealed normal tissue. Just as I begin to wonder if I'm going mad, they tell me the 'bad' news.

"We think you may have what's called an ectopic pregnancy."

Told you so, I think to myself.

This puts me in a whole new category of the failing to produce babies club. Apparently one in 100 pregnant women suffer ectopic pregnancies, where the embryo grows anywhere but the womb, and most often in one of the two fallopian tubes. The doctors agree that this time we might well be looking at some effect of my mother having taken the DES drug. The embryo could continue to grow in the tube until the tube bursts, at about seven to eight weeks of pregnancy. This means that a woman can bleed to death in a matter of hours, unless diagnosed and treated properly. That's the second bit of 'good news'. Apparently, I'm lucky because the embryo stopped growing of its own accord, and so rather than rupture the tube, it just damaged it, as a result of which I didn't bleed to death on the floor of the auction rooms or in my office.

I'll be back in surgery again by the end of the day, now for something called a laparoscopy, or key-hole surgery. They will make three or four incisions in my tummy, look at my tubes, fix what they need to fix, and stitch me up again. They assure me that I'll only be left with some tiny scars on my stomach and not to worry.

Fine, fine, I just go along with it all. I no longer feel in control of anything. Though relieved to finally know what's wrong, I just hand over to circumstances for now, and will digest this new bit of information and emotional upheaval another time. I have distanced myself from myself, because it's easier that way. I don't have to feel the pain, the fear, the sense of abandonment. I switch off, and to the outside world I appear brave.

For the third time in five weeks I am coming round from a general anaesthetic. My brain must have some pretty big blank areas in it by now, and I'm not sure it's doing me any good. What choice do I have though, I hardly feel like offering myself to the acupuncture community as a guinea pig for surgery under acupuncture. The muscles in my stomach are so sore. I feel like I've been doing a hundred sit-ups or something. I move about gingerly. The keyhole holes are indeed tiny, and the soreness is very different from the D&C.

The hardest thing is turning over in bed, and I spend the first night sitting half reclined and dozing. June says the soreness in my stomach will take about a week to go and to be aware of the fact that they have pumped loads of gas into my stomach to give them a bit more 'space' to work in during the operation. The gas will need to come out one way or the other over the next few days, so Peter had better be prepared! I manage a faint smile. He's in for some competition then.

In the car on the way home I manage a rather sick joke, saying to Peter how lucky he is to be taking home a burping and farting pregnancy failure who should count her lucky stars to be alive, and never mind about the baby. Peter gives me a sideways look, he's not used to me being sarcastic, and I'm not very good at it. I'm still holding back all my feelings, and keeping this stupidly brave face on the whole thing. It's not wrong, it's just that it's the only way I can survive this right now. What I need is for someone not to be fooled by my act, to gently see behind the mask, and non judgementally help me back to my real self and my real feelings again. I wear the mask too well though, even my nearest and dearest are fooled and I resent them for it.

"You have a thirty percent less chance of conceiving!" Whether it's the broad Scottish accent with which he delivers the statement, or the sheer insensitivity of the guy, the surgeon who speaks these words to me two weeks after the operation deserves to be shot. As soon as he drops this bombshell he reaches for his phone to answer his pager and excuses himself.

I suppose sheer brutality has had the same effect as the gentle sensitivity I craved from my nearest and dearest. The mask slips, the tears start to flow. I rush out of the consulting room to go and meet Peter at a restaurant by the canal. It's one thing losing another pregnancy, but the thought that now even becoming pregnant is going to be harder, is a real slap in the face. Why didn't they tell me this at the hospital two weeks ago. I came totally unprepared for anything other than a 'healing nicely, off you go' kind of thing. Not, you've a thirty percent less chance of conceiving.

As I walk into the restaurant the first thing I see is this incredibly pregnant woman sitting at a table opposite Peter. It's a conspiracy!

I refuse to sit where I can see her which means we move to a table outside. I'm also embarrassed about my tears, which now won't stop flowing. Peter suggests once again that we wait for a little while before we try for another baby. This time I agree, wondering if I ever want to try for another baby. What if next time my tube ruptures? The tears having subsided a bit we try to make some kind of battle plan. If I can't have any physical control over my reproductive organs, at least I can take some intellectual control, by finding the best specialist and sorting out once and for all where we stand. However, for now we will allow ourselves some time to regain our strength.

It's like a bad dream. Once again I'm becoming hyper sensitive to anything to do with pregnancies. I can't listen to relatives telling me about other pregnant family members and I hate them for even thinking that I'm interested. I've not spoken to my pregnant Dutch friends, who have almost all delivered at least one baby by now and one of whom is even pregnant with number two. I switch off any programme that has women falling happily pregnant and delivering perfect babies in the very next scene. I'm so hurt. I'm so angry. And I always end up taking it out on Peter. I'm not a very nice person to be with.

Everything I thought I had managed to deal with last summer is coming up again, and I'm not surprised to hear Peter say that maybe we should stop thinking and talking about babies altogether. The problem is, the feeling that I want to be a mum just won't go away. I want to but I can't stop thinking about it. This primal urge has me in its grip and I have no defence against it.

The Truth

What would you do, if I told you the truth.
If I told you straight, I'm not feeling great.
Hi, how are you, I'm fine, and you?

How would you cope, would you know what to say
If I broke with the custom, would you go away?
Hi, how are you, I'm fine, and you?

My pain is not casual, not an "Oh not so good,"
I'm mourning the loss of my motherhood.
Hi, how are you, I'm fine, and you?

Would it shock you to see me, dropping my mask
Behind which I hide, my pain, and my pride?
Hi, how are you, I'm fine, and you?

If only just someone, would reach for my hand,
just squeeze it and say, "I understand.....
I see through your mask, the pain and the pride,
I understand why you needed to hide.
I see that behind, that great happy smile,
is confusion and fear, but I am still here."

Just a squeeze in my hand, perhaps not even a word
just for someone to see, how much I hurt

Chapter 6

ENOUGH IS ENOUGH

We're taking a big break from the whole baby scene!!! I feel like broadcasting it to the world.... just so people won't ask. Not that they do, actually. I just imagine all these unasked questions, all these expectations, and do not have the ability to think to myself that they can all go to hell. Instead I feel obliged to explain where we're at and how we're doing. If I had kept my big mouth shut right from the start of this whole pregnancy business, I wouldn't feel now that I have all this explaining to do. Or perhaps I'm trying to do all this explaining because I don't really support the idea that we're taking a break. The part of me that is driven by the fear of a repeat ectopic, coupled with the attendant emotional upheaval, probably never wants to be pregnant again, but the part of me that longs to be a mother is still there. Underground, but still there.

At the next support group meeting I am welcomed back with care and consideration. When I tell them about my experiences of the last four weeks, they become really angry on my behalf. Blame the hospital, blame the doctors. Yet, I don't actually feel I have been badly treated, other than by the Scottish idiot. Of course, they might have suspected an ectopic pregnancy when I came back the second time, before subjecting me to the second D&C in a fortnight, but a lot of it is also misdirected anger, much like me taking my feelings out on Peter. That's a thought. Maybe I should start taking my frustrations out on the medical staff instead of on Peter. Give him a break.

Once I have said my piece the attention moves on to someone else. I realise that I am quite happy just sitting and listening to everyone. During the coffee break Tina is mentioned again. I am getting quite curious now. Somehow I have managed to miss her, at each of the two meetings I have attended, but who knows, I might meet her next time.

I decide to call the Miscarriage Association to see if they have more information about ectopic pregnancies and perhaps advice on treatment and prevention. As it turns out, they have very little information, but they do provide me with the name of someone in my area who has been through much the same shit as me, a miscarriage, and ectopic, and ...... a little girl! That last bit of information just to prove that eventually things can go right! When I write down her details I begin to laugh. Where have I heard this name before?

"Hi, my name is Lysanne, and I've been given your name by the Miscarriage Association."

"Oh yes, hang on, I'll just go and grab the other phone."

So far so good.

"Here I am again, so what happened to you?" her voice sounds really warm and caring.

"I had a miscarriage last year, and now I've just suffered an ectopic pregnancy. I heard you'd been through pretty much the same thing, and that you have a little girl..." my voice trailing off.

"Hannah. She's a little honey, and I feel very lucky to have her. But how are you feeling? It's so frightening to have an ectopic. Did you get rushed off to the hospital with a rupture?"

"No, I guess I was lucky," I say with hint of irony in my voice, "but it did take a couple of D&C's and some serious pain to find out what it was."

"It's really hard to diagnose, but that's still no excuse. I think there should be a national awareness campaign amongst all doctors so that any woman presenting with abdominal pain should be screened for pregnancy and an ectopic considered. It's frightening to think that women are still dying because of this."

I ignore the dying bit, "But you went on to have a baby, after an ectopic."

"That's right. I was looked after really well, and they can do a scan really early on in the pregnancy to see if it is in the right place or not. It doesn't stop you being scared as hell, but at least it helps if you feel you're in the right hands."

My sentiments exactly. We hit it off really well, and within minutes I feel like I'm talking to a friend. After a while we agree to meet up. Then, just before we hang up she tells me that not only does she have little Hannah, she is also five months pregnant.

"If that's hard for you right now, I really would understand."

But it's not. Funnily enough, I have no problem with the pregnancies of women who I know have suffered miscarriages and fertility problems. I only feel a sense of great hope and gladness that it is possible to go on and have children, and we make a date for the following week.

On my way to see Tina I become a little nervous. It turns out she lives in a sweet little cul-de-sac, just streets away from me. I decide to take my big old Dutch bicycle and as I pedal along the polluted Uxbridge Road I try to figure out why I feel so jittery. It's the idea that I'm going to go and meet someone to be helped, instead of to help, and it really feels quite alien. I shake myself. Silly thoughts, better to concentrate on finding her road. I balance the plant and the little present for her daughter as I swerve around the last corner and park the bike. Then I ring the bell and wait.

Tina opens the door and looks completely different from what I imagined. She is quite petite and has this wonderful big pregnant tummy sticking out in front of her, although I think she has tried to dress so that it doesn't show too much. I find I really don't mind. Her voice is as warm and friendly as it was on the phone, and somehow full of mischief. She sits me down in a chair and makes me a cup of tea.

"It's really weird that people don't seem to see this as a miscarriage. But in a way it feels worse than a miscarriage. It feels like I have been sent back to square one, and back some more. Not only am I no longer pregnant, but getting pregnant is now going to be harder too. It's so unfair." And I tell her about the guy who had told me about my reduced fertility.

Tina snorts, "I know him, there are far better people to see at the hospital than him. I'll put you in touch with them. But it's so true what you say. Until a few years ago nursing colleges didn't even teach that ectopic pregnancies were also experienced as miscarriages. You were assumed to be glad that you were still alive, never mind losing half your fertility, or the baby. Yet it's a double, triple blow."

"The nurses were actually really lovely. I met someone called June."

"Oh, she's a real honey too. You'll meet her at one of the support group meetings."

We talk some more about the shocking facts of ectopic pregnancies. I really was the lucky one. Some women are rushed to hospital by ambulance, go straight through to surgery, are cut open the old fashioned way to have their tube removed. No tiny scars, but a great big gash across your belly, and one less tube. Others, tragically, don't make it at all. Four to five women a year in Britain alone die of an undiagnosed or misdiagnosed ectopic pregnancy, making it the leading cause of pregnancy-related deaths in the first trimester. It's all very frightening and it makes me wonder how to cope if I ever get pregnant again.

"The most important thing is to make sure that you have a Consultant that you really trust. I know one of the Consultants whom you would get on with really well. If anyone gets you pregnant, it will be Mr. Wright. Why don't you give him a call just to see where you stand. Maybe there is a connection in all of this."

As I write down his number she repeats, "I'm sure Mr. Wright will help you to have a baby."

I giggle at the *double entendre*, and wonder how Peter would feel about that.

That afternoon I feel the beginnings of a wonderful friendship stirring. With tears in my eyes I touch her big tummy and see it as a sign of hope to all of us still waiting to carry our own precious cargo. Tina is funny, we laugh, at each other, and at ourselves, and we also weep for what is lost.

As I cycle home I shoot a little prayer of thanks heavenward. I'm deeply grateful for the support of women like Tina, women who I can identify with, who strengthen me. They are precious beyond words.

I have Mr. Wright's telephone number in my pocket. Now I'm part of a new kind of club. The *so we had a miscarriage but we're not going to let it beat us club*. I ring and make an appointment. The leaves have started to change colour but we are being treated to a wonderful Indian summer. At work I spend more time than I should composing a list of questions to ask Mr. Wright. I want to know if the ectopic and the first miscarriage are in any way connected to DES. The list is about ten questions long, so I hope Mr. Wright is a patient man. It feels good to be taking matters into my own hands, and to regain some manner of control over the situation. If I can't influence what my body does, at least I can try to exert some control over the process, and ensure that I'm getting the best medical help and support that I need.

Once more I mount my big black Dutch bicycle and make my way along the Uxbridge Road to the hospital. I've been told to go around to the side of the hospital where the private consulting rooms are, and to look for an inconspicuous green glass door. This is an experience in itself. Only in England, I think to myself, as I lean my old Dutch bike against the wall and cross from one world into another by just passing over the threshold from NHS to private healthcare. I panic as I open the door thinking about the old jeans and woolly sweater I'm wearing. Shouldn't I have dressed up properly first? Suddenly I'm quite nervous but a friendly smiling nurse instantly sits me down and offers me tea. There are beautiful paintings on the walls, a thick carpet underfoot, and soft music playing in the background. On the table lie scattered copies of 'Vogue', 'House & Garden', and of course 'Reader's Digest'.

I take it all in so that I can tell Peter about it later. I was the one who decided that I would go and see Mr. Wright on my own, part of the new 'Lysanne in control' regime, and just sitting here in the hospital's private waiting room is soothing.

I deserve a bit of pampering. I need looking after, although the very person who wants to look after me is being shut out. I understand it even less than Peter does, but we're just not very happy at the moment. We try so hard, but it feels as if we're speaking two different languages, and they're not Swedish or Dutch!

Mr. Wright looks a bit like a friendly garden gnome, with the kindest, most open face. He meets me at the door of his consulting room and we shake hands. In that one handshake he restores something that had been lost to me in the latest round of fun and games at the hospital. I become a person again, not a sick object in the hands of other people. It does me good to feel I'm being seen as a real person, a whole person, not just a patient with something wrong that needs fixing.

"Peter and I want to have a bit of a break, so we're not going to try to get pregnant right now. I just wanted to get some clarity to help me make up my mind about the next step."

"Is there anything in particular you want to ask?"

Flushing scarlet I gingerly pull out my list, one copy for me, one copy for him. Now what will he say?

"Oh good, I like lists," and he compliments me on having the foresight to bring him his own copy.

"Could there be a link between the two miscarriages? My mother was prescribed DES when she was carrying me. Is there any chance the problems are being caused by that?"

"No, as far as I can see from your notes, the only link between the two events is sheer bad luck," but he says it with compassion, as if to soften the words.

"So what are my chances of having another ectopic?"

"Normally, these random ectopics occur on average in 1 out of 100 pregnancies, although the instance might be higher for DES daughters. However, having suffered one ectopic pregnancy the chances of having another are one in ten."

"So if I was to have ten more pregnancies, one of them might be ectopic?" I say, trying to get it straight in my head. Statistics never were my strongest subject at school.

"In a way.... You could also say for every pregnancy you have, there is a ten percent risk that it will be ectopic."

That sounds less worrying. If someone told me I had a ten percent chance of failing an exam, I would laugh it off, study like mad, and pass with flying colours. I guess the problem is you can't study for having a good pregnancy. Also, what are odds? In the end, what happens, happens, and you can't do a thing about it.

"Your left tube looks fine, and apart from the trauma of having the ectopic removed, which was close to the ovary, the right tube is not too bad either."

"Is it worth doing a dye test to see if the right tube is blocked?" I ask, using my new found intelligence from the support group.

"Since you're not planning a pregnancy right now, I think we should leave well enough alone. Let's see if a healthy pregnancy manages to pop through of it's own accord. I'd rather not be too invasive."

I agree, especially since I don't feel ready for more white coats just now, even in the shape of Mr. Wright. Question six, and he is still as patient and as committed as when we began. "What happens should, if, I get pregnant again?" This is the question I'm dreading, since I don't really want to think about that, yet, but forewarned is forearmed and Mr. Wright takes the time to explain.

"When you next fall pregnant, an early scan would show at six weeks whether the embryo was 'in viro', that's to say, in the womb. If it's in the right place, hurrah, we go on from there."

"And if it's not?"

"If there continues to be no evidence of an embryo in the womb and you remain pregnant, then there is likely to be another ectopic pregnancy in the making. Using the same procedure as before, the pregnancy would then be removed before it can cause any damage."

Forever resourceful I ask, "Is there no way of letting the ovum be fertilised, after it's made its way through the tube?" My faith in modern medicine verging on the miraculous.

A smile plays around his lips, "I'm afraid that is not possible, but it's quite a wonderful idea."

We talk about a new technique that Tina mentioned, where some doctors inject a substance into the pregnancy that terminates it, so that it doesn't even need to be removed from the tube. New techniques are being practised all the time, and the answer seems to be, if you're vigilant, and you have the proper kind of medical help, the risk of bleeding to death on an operating table is actually very small. It all seems very straightforward and clear-cut, and in a way, having another ectopic, under these 'controlled' circumstances, would be preferable to me than having another miscarriage at three months. What am I saying? Having a healthy pregnancy would be the most preferable option of course, one that I tend to forget still exists.

As I stand by the door to take my leave I just about manage to resist the urge to give him a big hug. Instead I pump his hand up and down with heartfelt enthusiasm. I feel so much better after this visit. As I pump away at his hand he says: "Take care now, and see you in the Spring."

Who said anything about coming back in the Spring? It occurs to me to say that we might wait a lot longer than that before we try again, but what the heck, I'm out of the door already.

Armed with all this knowledge I feel stronger to face another pregnancy. I feel I now know how to ask for the best care for myself, and ensure that I'm on top of the medical process, not running one step behind. I feel empowered, and Mr. Wright encourages that feeling. There is a lot of good news to take home with me. I have a very healthy left tube, a ninety percent chance of a healthy pregnancy, and the opportunity to stay with Mr. Wright as his patient! I call Peter and then my mother to tell them how happy I am after the visit. Mamma is perhaps a little disappointed that there won't yet be any further investigations, but she is happy that I sound so happy, and, after all, that is all that matters. Peter is also happy for me, but feels less and less part of the whole process. More like a sperm donor than a husband. There is so much distance.

When you buy a bright red overcoat, you suddenly see everyone else wearing bright red overcoats because somehow your antenna is tuned in to it. When you lose a pregnancy, your antenna is tuned to pick out every single pregnant woman in the street, whether you want to or not, and there are loads. I really do wonder what God is up to. I meet the most wonderful women at the miscarriage group, who would make the most caring dedicated mothers, dutifully giving up smoking and drinking, taking their iron pills, only to have their hopes dashed again and again. Is there actually some sort of greater plan, or is it purely a question of physical factors. Sperm meets ovum, merges, creates zygote, starts to divide and becomes embryo. If it doesn't manage the job, it packs it in, and starts again. That's the medical bit, the bit that keeps questions about spirit and soul out of the equation.

Doctors who think it is silly to say to women that they have lost a baby are hung up on the fact that in their eyes, this 'product of conception' was never a baby. What they forget is that for the mother-to-be the baby is more alive in her head in the first three months, than in her tummy. The moment you test positive, in your mind and in your heart the notion of a baby grows, even though the corresponding physical process in your womb, if you're lucky, has only reached the foetal stage. This is where so many misunderstandings spring from.

The question that I find I need to answer for myself is more to do with the notion of when Life begins, when the soul comes into it? Contrary to most women, I don't experience my two losses as the actual losses of a baby, or a child. If anything, more as the loss of the opportunity to have one. Before the miscarriages, I used to think Life is sparked the moment the sperm and the egg melt together, but now I wonder. Biological life, yes, but spiritual life? What kind of life, whose life? Without the life giving force of the mother, the embryo wouldn't survive. It cannot yet think, or reason, or record thoughts and feelings in its brain, or can it? The brainstem, the deepest most hidden part of the brain is formed in the first weeks, and it's from there that our ability to consciousness originates. The cortex, the bit that regulates our acquired knowledge and information, is formed much later. Yet we need to be able to know we are conscious, to be able to know we are alive. So what determines life? Breathing? A heart beat? The ability to register thoughts and experiences?

One evening an image comes to me of my womb being like a great big building site. The egg and the sperm are the building materials with which to build a secure home, but no one will live there until it's complete. If the materials are sound, if my body executes the contract on time, the house will be built, and a new soul moves in. So what happens if the materials are not sound, and the builder does not execute the contract correctly? The whole process just has to start again. At some stage, when it's clear that the body is a good, sound and safe dwelling, a soul moves into it. Perhaps it's already been sitting in some kind of heavenly waiting room where time does not exist. It's been sitting there waiting through two miscarriages now, that little soul meant for us, and once my womb houses a sound body, that little soul will move in. The image works for me and makes me feel calm and peaceful inside. Hang in there little soul, the time will come.....

What I mourn is the fact that I'm not a very good builder. Perhaps my building site is a little rocky. Perhaps the material that Peter and I bring to the site is not what it could be. Perhaps my mourning is coming to terms with failure, something I'm not used to, something that takes humility to accept. I also mourn the loss of status that goes with losing a pregnancy. A pregnant woman is the toast of the town, special, to be cherished. You touch her belly fleetingly, as if to pick up something of the miracle that is developing inside her. Being pregnant is being in a state so blessed, and so special, the world seems to lie at your feet. And when you're knocked from your pedestal, it hurts!

Until now I had been able to set my hand at anything I wanted. I'm reasonably bright, a good organiser, and a hard worker. I also manage to bullshit my way into a great many situations, without thinking how I'm going to get myself out of them again later. Yet Mother Nature has decided these attributes do not apply to the process of making babies. This is not something I can fix, it's about waiting and seeing. What will come will come.

Pappa likened my intense broodiness, which had started the year after our wedding, to the way in which I would always try, as a little girl, to climb the tree that was just that little bit too high for me, or the fence that was just too slippery. Undaunted I would go at the task with all my energy and enthusiasm, and unfailingly, I would land on earth with a resounding bang. Was I trying to 'become a mother' before it was my time? What about all those other women then, those who didn't even want it to be their time yet. We're back to the old question again, is there really a master plan up there, or is it just the luck of the draw?

Frankly, I'm growing too tired of trying to second guess life's existential questions, and so the act of humility is also an act of throwing my hands up in the air and saying very loudly; "What the hell, I don't know," hoping that someone up there does. I'm in a more reflective state of mind, resigned to the fact that for us childbearing is not a straightforward matter. I'm good at a lot of things, but having babies is just not turning out to be my forte. It helps to mentally break the process down, into easy manageable chunks. Once we are ready, and that is a question in itself, our main aim is to have a lot of fun trying to get pregnant. Then, with each month of early pregnancy, there will be hurdles to overcome. I'm willing to face them and to try to overcome them, not gladly, but understanding that for once in my life, I'm really going to have to fight for something. If we still want a baby that is, since I am not even sure about that anymore.

Peter and I want to wait and turn our minds completely away from the whole baby issue until something tells us we're ready. We realise that we need time to get back on our feet as a couple. The past eighteen months have been tough on our relationship. I need to stop blaming Peter for not being inside my head the whole time and reading me like a book, and he agrees that he needs to try to be a little less solution oriented and more sensitive. A cuddle instead of trying to fix things which can't be fixed.

We love each other so much, it's about time we started showing it again. Time to start living again. and trusting that Life will decide what's best for us.

Chapter 7

A new beginning

Christmas and New Year have been and gone and we have two feline additions to the family, Badger and Bundy. If, for now, we're not going to shower our parenting feelings onto a child of our own, we might as well practise on a pair of kittens. I pick them up from the local vet who tells me they were rescued from the rubbish tip by a kind lady from Hayes. They're absolutely gorgeous and lie curled up in a white furry ball behind the books on the bookshelf. Kind, well-meaning people suggest thoughtfully that perhaps we got them because we weren't having any luck with children of our own.

Peter was not too keen on the cats at first, but a month after they arrive on our doorstep, I overhear him telling cat stories at a dinner party ... what a pushover. He is telling them about the state of war that we appear to be living through at the moment. Feline war, that is. After about a month Badger and Bundy no longer curl up in a furry ball behind the books, and instead are increasingly nasty to each other, fighting like mad. Well, who said that siblings always get on? I ask the vet about their behaviour as we come in for their next jabs. It does make me feel a little bit like 'playing at parents', but what the hell.

"Are Badger and Bundy going through some kind of adolescent stage?"

The vet assures me that they are actually quite grown up by now, and that they are trying to figure out who is dominant. Unless they become a danger to each other we are to let them get on with it. Sure enough, after another two weeks we notice they have reached some kind of stalemate or truce, with Badger living upstairs and Bundy occupying the downstairs living area. The kitchen seems to be the neutral territory where they are fed and watered. This is how it stays, two equally dominant females, deciding to divvy up the house rather than fight over it. Quite a story, and much more fun than first gurgles and nappies!

I truly feel I'm ready to start living again. New diaries, new calendars. Out with the old, in with the new. The new me. No more moping about feeling either a failure or a mother spurned. Time to start a new phase in my life. For years now I've felt that being a journalist was not at all fulfilling. I wanted to do more to really put something back into life. My own recent spate of emotional upheaval has taught me how important it is to have people out there who don't only care, but also have the professional skills to support someone.

I have always been a 'helper', now I've experienced what it is like to 'be helped', and my thoughts have been turning to how I can make my career move. Coming from a family of academics, the expected thing would be to go back to university and study psychology. However, that didn't work for journalism, spending years studying to become a journalist and then finding out it wasn't really my thing. So this time round I'm doing it the Lysanne way, bottom up. Find out if I'm actually cut out for that kind of work, whether it would be as fulfilling as I think, and then taking the next step.

Georgy lends me the autobiography of Chad Varah, the founder of the Samaritans, and I'm really inspired, especially by the way in which he describes being 'led' without actually understanding what it was that was being expected of him.

Of course I start to notice the little sign in Uxbridge shopping centre pointing to the Samaritans, but really, it does seem to be pointing the way ahead for me. They have a short but intense training course after which you commit to one afternoon or morning a week and one overnight. Peter is extremely positive about the whole thing, and I suppose, relieved that I seem to be getting back on my feet again. It's not the first time I have thought about a career change, but I always coupled it to the time when I would be at home with children. Studying, as well as spending a lot of time with them. I felt frustrated because I thought that one thing was holding the other back, but then it suddenly dawned on me; I can start making the change right now! It was only in my own fantasy that I had it linked to a certain phase in my life.

Steaming ahead with my plans finally makes me realise how in the past two years everything had become 'baby' oriented. There was not one other area in my life that was developing and growing. Everything was on hold for the big 'baby' thing to happen. Now that things are on the move again, it feels great!

I guess I have learned some pretty big lessons in the past two years, and gained a little more compassion both for others, and for myself. I now know from my own experience that it's not okay to try to cope with everything by being strong and not sharing it with anyone. And failure's not such a disaster either, it's an opportunity for growth, although I still need to work on that one!! If I volunteer as a Samaritan, or, in the future, work as a counsellor, it's a message that I can help other people find for themselves, allowing them to move on in life like I feel I've been able to. I feel hope and excitement for the future, good things are going to come out of it, but they are no longer automatically linked to having babies.

Last week we were in New York, and I popped over to see my colleagues in Washington. In April we are going to California, where I'll join Peter on a shoot, tagging on an extra week's holiday, maybe in San Francisco, and it feels great that we can do all these things. Friendly neighbours will feed the cats, we lock the door and off we go, not tied down by anything or anyone. So different compared to friends who are bogged down with babies in carrycots and nappy bags slung around their necks. We can celebrate our freedom from parenthood, for now, and so what if we are a little smug about it all. No 'smugger' than the few former acquaintances who have dangled their babies in front of our noses like some coveted prize, and whom we quietly dropped from our Christmas list. The quiet voices that long to be part of the far more exclusive club of parents are stilled. We won't hear them any longer. We're living it up.

Having really made the commitment to be together, the romance is well and truly coming back into our lives. Peter is still travelling a lot, but his homecomings are full of joy. Last week he came home early in the morning from a transatlantic flight to find me sitting in the bath.

As usual I was being watched by Bundy, the upstairs cat, who I'm convinced was a sexual delinquent in a previous life. Peter's look of sheer delight was a joy to behold. Suffice to say he made himself quite at home again and after a moment or two Bundy left the bathroom in disgust, tail high with indignation. Having too much fun to take precautions, we don't. Some quick, and probably under the circumstances far from reliable mental arithmetic, tells me I should be over the tricky part of my cycle by now anyway. What a super, wonderful, lovely morning, neither of us feel like going to work afterwards. However, duty calls and with a long loving kiss we say goodbye for the day.

We talk again in the afternoon. Spring is in the air, and we're so in love. Just cooing at each other on the phone like we did when we first met. All the times that I've screamed at him for not understanding what I was going through, for not taking charge, not taking care of me the way I expected him to. It makes me blush with shame. And yet he just accepts me as I am, glad to have me back, warts and all, for better or worse. Lucky old me. Even if we are never to have a family together, I feel convinced we would manage to make something good come out of it. It just seems such a special day today, as if every tree and every flower has a smile on its face. Oh hell, what am I talking about, it's just the aftermath of good sex!

Sunday morning we have a lazy breakfast in bed, trying to read the Sunday papers without the cats sitting on them, and making snide remarks about all our friends who have no doubt been up bleary eyed and bad tempered since six o'clock this morning with their screaming brats. Later today we might visit the garden centre to buy some plants for the garden. We want to make it look really nice for the summer, so that we can spend hours just sitting in it and enjoying the colours. Perhaps we might even paint the fence. Then again, we might decide to move house after the summer, and then we'll put our energy into that. The world's our oyster and we can do what we like with it. There is nothing holding us back. Of course somewhere in the back of my mind it has registered that today is Mother's Day, but it's not until we get to the garden centre that I realise the effect that it might have on me. Like the drip, drip, drip of a small stream whittling away at a rock, the significance of the day slowly starts to filter up from my unconscious mind. Everything we see around us celebrates motherhood; Mother's Day cards, Mother's Day bouquets, Mother's Day balloons, and in the midst of it all, mothers, grandmothers, families, babies. STOP.

Wrong Place!

It's a bit like a volcano. You think it's dead, but somewhere deep inside, the hot molten rock is still rumbling, waiting for a weak moment to come bursting out through the thin unhealed crust above. The more you put the lid on, the bigger the pressure, and suddenly, right there in the garden centre, I explode. I take the entire tray of pansies that we've bought and smash them onto the ground in the car park. Then I get in the car and start bawling my eyes out. I just want everyone and everything to go away and leave me alone!

When, oh when is this madness going to go away. I'm so completely fed up with myself. I'm split in half. Part of me happy with our decision to put the whole baby thing on hold, and another part of me, first silently, now violently, demanding attention for this primordial urge to become a mother. To fulfil my biological function on this planet. Forget careers, ambition, glass ceilings and breaking through them, a woman's body is tied up with the process of procreation from the moment we start having our monthly bleeds. I can't deny myself this primal instinct, and yet I wish, I wish, that it would just go away and leave me alone.

Peter tries to salvage what is left of the pansies and as I watch his strained face in the rear mirror my heart reaches out to him. I hate myself for the pain I'm causing, and the confusion in his eyes when from one moment to the next I turn from strong and confident, into a wobbling wreck. In his wedding speech, held a lifetime ago, he'd said that amongst all the other things he loved about me, the best thing was the fact that I was so unpredictable. I somehow don't think this display of unbridled emotion was quite what he had in mind.

We drive home in silence. As usual Peter has one hand on the wheel and the other on my knee. I just stare out of the window. I'm so confused, so fed up, too angry to cry and too sad to be angry. What a waste of a good day.

Later we talk about the outburst. Perhaps I am not really happy with our decision to drop the baby thing. Have I been trying to fool myself, to please Peter, who has really gone off the idea? Can't I even trust myself anymore when I feel good and positive like I have been doing for the past weeks? Is everything a sham? I don't know, I just don't know anymore. Peter's questions exhaust me. My own questions exhaust me. I just want to go back to bed and be back where we were this morning.

What I haven't told Peter is that I've realised my mental arithmetic of a few weeks ago was seriously off, and our bathroom session fell slap bang in the middle of my cycle. I don't really want to share my suspicions with anyone yet, 'cause I feel such an idiot, but I'm thinking of popping into town for a blood test. I call various family planning clinics and I find one that will do the test for me. Perhaps the outburst in the garden centre might have had more to do with hormones than with emotions.

Of course I could go to Dr. Walker, or even Mr. Wright, but for some reason I'm embarrassed to. We've been so certain about not wanting to try for another baby right now, I can't bear the thought of admitting that we've slipped up. It seems so irresponsible. I know the sensible thing would be just to wait and see if I get my period, but I don't want to wait until then. If I'm late, I have to wait even longer to find out if I'm pregnant. So much for trusting Life...

The next day at the clinic it takes a few goes to explain that I'm not yet even late with my period, but that I'm worried and have a history of ectopics. On a rational level I know that even if I was pregnant, and it was ectopic, I still wouldn't have anything to worry about, but I feel panic-stricken and want to know, NOW. Perhaps this is why I don't want to go to Dr. Walker, I feel a bit of a panic merchant. And yet, panic is what I feel. I believe a blood test will tell me with all certainty whether I'm pregnant or not, so that I don't have to go through the process of counting the days should I be late. If I'm pregnant, I want to know ASAP. If I'm not, I can just heave a sigh of relief and forget all about it. Have my period, hug my hot water bottle, and live on. The fact that a gloriously romantic sexy morning is becoming the source of a renewed attack of panic and worry makes me mad!

So get a grip, I tell myself, *stop being such a drama queen.*

Oh that I could, I would. I really would!

Taking blood only takes a few minutes. Then I wander around the back streets of Tottenham Court Road. Two hours, she said, then I could come back for the results, unless I wanted to call. I wander around aimlessly, buy a teapot, and imbue it with some kind of mystical power. I toy with the idea of pregnancy, then reject it again, and firmly pass by the doors of Mothercare. It seems there is no room in my brain for any thoughts that have no bearing on the state of either being, or not being, pregnant.

How did I get here again? I was so happy to have moved on from this total obsession. I chide myself for being so careless, and at the same time refrain from buying a slinky summer dress. Well, you never know. After half an hour of this aimless wandering about I decide to take the tube home and call the clinic instead. At least I can try to get some work done while I'm at home. As if ...

When I pick up the phone two hours later I try to sound as businesslike as possible, as does the woman on the other end. The answer is no, the test was negative. I'm not pregnant. A mixture of relief and disappointment rushes through me as I sit holding the phone. The nurse at the other end asks me once more if it was really ten days since we made love, as more recent dallying could make the test unreliable. I nod to myself, yes, yes. Well, it was 10 days ago, wasn't it? I feel a little numb, very stupid, and as elated as I feel disappointed. I would have been quite chuffed I suppose, but I'm also extremely relieved not to be back on that roller-coaster. Not for now anyway.

Just to prove me wrong about rushing off and wasting fifty quid on a blood test, my pre-period pains start the very next day. That whole blood test idea was a bit silly. I might as well have waited another few days and let Mother Nature tell me herself. My father's words about my childhood impatience and rushing at fences come back to me in a flash. I manage a compassionate giggle at myself. When will I learn?

My periods have been getting more and more painful since the miscarriages. First comes a lower back ache to herald the imminent arrival of yet another session in a hot bath and snuggled up to a hot water bottle, and then all hell breaks loose. I've read somewhere that

Rosemary tea helps the womb to contract more easily and so relieves some of the period pain. I haven't been to the shops so I search around for some dried herbs instead. I make an infusion with some very old herbs I find lying at the back of the cupboard. I've also been prescribed some medication by Dr. Walker which I'm supposed to take a few days before my period starts.

Since I know I'm not pregnant I wash the pills down with the Rosemary brew and bunker up for the night. A few years ago my flatmate and I had 'synchronised' periods. One night we came on almost simultaneously and we sat on her bed, wrapped up in her duvet, passing a hot water bottle from left to right, and a whisky bottle from right to left. Our male flatmate occasionally managed to make a successful grab for the whisky bottle, as he ran up and down the stairs to boil the kettle to top up the scorching hot water bottle. Braced for the worst I wait for my period to come.

Either the herbal brew is doing overtime, or the pills have discouraged any blood flow, but after fours days I'm still waiting. It's a good thing that I know I'm not pregnant, or else I would have been in a real state. Now I'm just feeling bemused. I wonder if drinking all that Rosemary tea before my period has actually somehow made it go away altogether. That would be nice, although I'm getting sick and tired of my female parts acting weirdly. They seem to keep themselves well and truly in the centre of attention, even though I would rather they didn't. I'm totally and utterly confused.

Peter knows about the trip up to London and says he doesn't trust the test. He has to go away to a conference in Paris next week but he really wants me to make an appointment with Mr. Wright. I'd rather not bother anyone with this, since it means I'll also have to explain about my clandestine trip up to town, about which I feel more and more stupid. Then Peter points out that as a private patient, a paying private patient, I would be doing Mr. Wright a favour by coming to see him, since he would not be able to make a living if everybody decided not to bother him. He's right I suppose, and it does feel easier to be paying my way, rather than being at the mercy of the system. So I call, but the earliest appointment I can make is the day after Peter leaves for Paris. It's a shame but I'm fine going on my own. After all, it's not as if I'm going there to find out if I'm pregnant.

Still no period, which now makes me more than a week late. My appointment with Mr. Wright is tomorrow and I decide I might as well bring a urine sample. I rifle through the kitchen cupboards to find a suitable container. To my shame I have to admit that I'm not a very environmentally friendly person, recycling every pot and tin. I tend to just chuck everything into the big black hole under the sink. I find it makes for very tidy kitchen cupboards but nothing useful to put a wee sample in. I continue my search in the bathroom and there my eye falls on the basket with the totally useless collection of miniature hotel shampoo bottles that Peter insists on bringing back with him from every trip. Now they finally come in useful. I rinse one out, run it with the dishes in the dishwasher, and then leave it prominently on the shelf by the toilet to remind me to fill it with a sample in the morning. Well.... a sample'ette; it's only a miniature!

The private consulting rooms have the same effect on me as last time. I feel cosseted, spoiled and well looked after. I'm provided with a nice cup of coffee in a bone china cup, and last autumn's art exhibition has been replaced with paintings of a nautical nature. I pick up a 'Homes & Gardens' and look at the beautiful photographs of spring garden displays. Suddenly the garden centre scene replays itself in my head. I stare over the top of my magazine – what is going on?

Across from me a couple wait for their turn. I miss Peter. Why did he have to go off and do so much travelling this spring. I'm reminded again of his happy homecoming, and a light smile plays on my lips. The female half of the couple gives me a bitchy look. Probably thinks

I'm flirting with her husband. I direct my absent minded stare somewhere else, somewhere safer. I'm far too distracted to read. I feel worried and yet I also feel like giggling. I wish I wasn't alone though. Perhaps I should have brought one of the cats.

The couple opposite me are called in, and a deep silence descends on the waiting room. I need the toilet, but I decide to save it. I finger the miniature shampoo bottle in the pocket of my cardigan. Again this idiotic smile plays around my lips.

Then it's my turn to go in. Again it's the firm handshake and a cheerful nice to see you again. I'm instantly at ease. Mr. Wright gets out his little laptop and starts tapping in my details. Once he has retrieved me from his laptop we go through the events of the past two weeks; romantic morning, garden centre, blood test, not pregnant, the herbal teas, the painkillers and Peter telling me I should come and see Mr. Wright. He listens patiently, smiles at my reference to Peter's happy homecoming, and shakes his head when I tell him I feel stupid about the blood test. I conclude this grand summing up with the words: "I know I'm not pregnant, but I haven't started my period, so now what's going on?"

"Perhaps it might be a good idea to repeat the blood test, unless of course ..." I pull the miniature shampoo bottle from my pocket like a magician pulls a rabbit from a hat.

"Hhrrumph," I hear, as he leaves the room, and I think he is amused.

Now the room has gone very quiet. Mr. Wright has taken the sample to the little lab at the back of the consulting rooms. I hear him talk softly with the sister in charge. I look at the trees in the park behind the consulting rooms, just about to come into leaf. I hear children playing in the playground, an ambulance racing by, a fly buzzing away at the window. A lump is starting in my throat, and it is as if time herself is standing still. What if ...

The door opens behind me. A hand on my shoulder, a chuckle, "Well done, you're pregnant."

It's the well done that gets me, the lump in my throat grows to the size of a brick, and hot tears well up in my eyes and roll down my cheeks. Well done, he says, making me feel that in all the failure of the past year or so, I've finally managed to get something right. I think about calling Peter, pappa and my mother, Tina, and Georgy. They'll be so confused, the whole idea was not to have a baby for the time being, how will I explain that we fucked up, so to say. And yet my next thought is, who cares, who cares what others think, I'm pregnant, I'm really pregnant.

I might have been sitting there for an hour, or five minutes, and judging from the look on Mr. Wright's face, it wouldn't have mattered either way. Sitting opposite me he beams, you might even think he is the one who is pregnant. That is what makes him so special, he reflects your feelings in the most remarkable way. I sit there and I stare back at him and finally a large grin starts to spread across my face. I find my voice, "well fancy that ..."

I was right about the hormonally induced temper tantrum at the Garden Centre. And what a waste of time doing that blood test. Suddenly I think of all the herbal stuff I've been taking to stop the period pain that was never even going to come, and the painkillers. What if I've already done something to harm the pregnancy. What about the trip to America? As the news slowly sinks in, a thousand worries clamour for attention in my brain, and I start to panic.

"Alright?"

I look up, and again see Mr. Wright's still beaming face and feel a great sense of trust and security. Things will be fine, I'm in good hands, I'll be well looked after, whatever happens. Mr. Wright patiently goes through each and every one of my fears. The painkillers and the herbal remedies will most likely not have had any effect on the pregnancy. The blood test, well, they aren't always 100% correct, but at least it got me through the first week of being pregnant without knowing it and so without worrying about it. And that takes us to the next step. I have another week ahead of me before I know if the pregnancy is in the proper place and Mr. Wright books me in for a scan in a week's time. At that point I'll be six weeks pregnant and the sack should be visible in the womb, or not.

If it's in the womb, great. If not, well, I know the procedure, and there would not yet be any risk of the pregnancy rupturing my tube. So I just sit tight for the next week, hope for the best, and trust that things are going to be alright. Another strong handshake and I'm on my way.

I walk out into the sunshine and suddenly remember how last autumn Mr. Wright had said: "See you in the Spring." Either this man has a direct line to God, or words spoken by him take on a greater meaning. Funny how there seem to be little 'signs' around to tell me this pregnancy is good. I cycle home in a daze.

I'm sitting in the conservatory with Badger and a cup of tea when the phone rings. It's Peter. No point beating about the bush. I tell him at once that I'm pregnant. It goes very, very quiet at the other end of the line. I know the news is received with mixed feelings. It's not about whether he wants to be a dad or not, but he was just starting to get his life back, and more importantly, his wife back, and he knows the consequences of another failure. He too is scared, scared for what might happen to this pregnancy, scared for what might happen to us. He finally says that he doesn't know what to say. He's happy, but also scared. He suggests we try not to talk about it until he is home. And we hang up.

In the past months his colleagues have been becoming dads by the dozen, and once I asked him how that made him feel. He said it felt like all these guys were getting this great sports car apart from him, and he didn't know why. I know now that he has also been hurt by the previous two fiascos, as well as having to put up with how it affected me. I love him for being so sincere and true to his feelings. It gives me permission to also be in two minds about the whole thing. He will be home in a day and it's right that we decide to try to think about other things in the meantime. But in the meantime...

I meet him at the airport. We give each other a big bear hug and a long, long cuddle. On the way home in the car we don't talk, we just sit and hold hands. Our mantra becomes whatever happens, we had a wonderful morning, and no one is going to take that away from us. The other thing we realise is how easily I got pregnant, never mind 'you have a forty percent less chance of conceiving'.

Who do we tell? I remember vowing that I wasn't going to tell a soul next time, not until I was at least six months pregnant. But we want to tell our innermost circle of friends, Tina of course, and Georgy. People at work need to know we are going into another 'unreliable' phase again, perhaps having to dash off to the hospital like a few months ago. We try to be positive, but we do seem to allow more thought for what to do when things go wrong, rather than when things go right. The one thing I won't discuss or even think about is the question "when is the baby due?" I'm not having a baby, I'm just pregnant. And that's all we can deal with right now. We decide not to tell our parents, since we know how much they have worried about us before. They can't do anything, and it will be better to wait until we can give them some good news.

The week passes at an excruciatingly slow pace. Every morning I wake up thinking, *one more night passed off without a crisis,* and I'm not even two months pregnant yet! This is the tragedy of miscarriages.

A pregnancy – at least in the early stages – will never be that source of unadulterated joy again. Being pregnant becomes synonymous with being scared, being vulnerable, and having your hopes on a very low pitch, for fear of having them dashed. You try to relax, and yet you feel you need to be on guard the whole time to make sure nothing is going to go wrong. As if you can stop anything from going wrong. Very deep inside flickers a candle of hope, a flame of trust, and it's that which helps me to get through the week to the day of the first scan.

Thankfully it's been booked for first thing in the morning, and we drive there holding our breath. I have an overnight bag in the trunk, just in case I need to stay in for an operation. Joy and pain, hope and despair are all vying for a place in my heart right now. Just before we walk through the door we take a deep breath, look each other deep in the eyes as we whisper our mantra; *"at least we had a great morning, and at least we know you can fall pregnant easily, and no one is going to take that away from us."*

We hold hands and in we go. I don't have to drink litres of water since it's a vaginal scan and you actually need a really empty bladder. It's more accurate and a better way to pick up the tiny sack that might be floating about in my womb. I lie down on the bed, Peter sits next to me, and the usual blue crocheted NHS blanket is laid over my lower half for modesty's sake. Mr. Wright comes in and watches as the radiographer focuses the image on the screen. They exchange a smile, and then she points out something to Mr. Wright who nods and says,

"It's there! It's in the womb, congratulations."

All in all it has taken less than two minutes, but I feel I've just lived through a lifetime. I'm so happy I'm ready to explode. First hurdle overcome. How I have dreamed about hearing those words in the past seven days. Peter and I clutch one another's hands as we nod excitedly at the inexplicable grey and black fuzz on the screen that has just revealed the mystery of a new life growing inside me. The fuzz is printed out and with the first picture of our pregnancy we go to meet Mr. Wright back in his office.

Sister is beaming, Mr. Wright is beaming, and Peter and I are still holding hands. Mr. Wright points out the details of the scan picture and with a little imagination we can see the tiny sack in the womb. A year ago I didn't even know that a fertilised egg could end up anywhere other than in the right place. Now I feel as if Peter and I have cleared a major hurdle, and we are so proud. Bamboozled, but proud. We add another line to our mantra; *"at least we know it can end up in the right place. And no one, absolutely no one, is going to take that away from us."*

Mamma knows something is up the moment I tell her our trip to America is cancelled. There is no way I'm going to risk anything with this pregnancy, least of all a plane journey. I've never been very good at lying to her, but if she does suspect something, she is wisely waiting for me to tell her in my own time.

Little gets past her. Even with the North Sea between us she intuitively knows what her child needs from her. I want to be a mother just like that, and I can't believe that unwittingly I'm once again back in the race. We are taking it one day at a time, one step at a time. We have a grip on our feelings and emotions, and brace ourselves for another bout of disappointment and pain. And yet, and yet, a little voice somewhere says things will be fine.

Only two days after the scan the euphoria has worn off and I'm beset by worry. I try to put the whole thing out of my mind. The next scan won't be for two weeks, the stage at which a repeat of the blighted ovum, cause of miscarriage no.1, can be eliminated. Will there be a heartbeat?

Tina is away on holiday, about the worst timing ever. Georgy and I meet up at our favourite Sushi restaurant. At first we try to avoid the subject, and then, failing miserably, talk about it all night. It's good to share my fears with her, as well as my hopes, and to know that she doesn't judge me for being fickle and thinking first one thing and then another. She is a good, patient friend and listens as I ramble on about scans and percentages. I already know who the Godmother is going to be. *Stop it Lysanne, don't think like that!* I immediately pull myself up short. Anything that might be construed as assuming things will be fine is tempting the devil. A healthy dose of humility and fatalism keeps the gods at bay!

Outwardly life seems to just go on as normal, day follows day, week follows week. My boss comes over from the States to speak at a conference. He also wants to discuss a major new project with me, with big implications for the future. I'm absolutely honest with him, even though I know it could cost me the opportunity of working on this new project. He and his wife suffered a miscarriage a few years ago, and so I know he is sensitive to the subject. I'm a bundle of joy and fear as I tell him about the scans and the fact that another ectopic is at least ruled out. He orders me a big glass of orange juice and instead of talking business we talk families.

The only way Peter can cope with the pregnancy is to try to avoid talking about it as much as possible, avoiding it, blocking it out. Not because he doesn't want me to be pregnant, but because he is so scared of us getting our hopes up. By just pretending it's not there, he thinks he won't miss it when it's gone. Thank goodness I have Georgy and Tina to talk to, as well as the women at the miscarriage group. His way is to look after me, fussing around like a mother hen. It's just that he can't sit down and talk about how scared we both are.

Of course sex has gone out the window again, along with the personal trainer I had recently hired to help get me back into shape. I know it won't harm the pregnancy, but if things do go wrong I don't want to have any sticks to beat myself with. Paté, soft cheese, it's all on the banned list, and from the moment we knew the pregnancy was in the womb I stopped smoking again. My only vice is sushi, which is full of healthy proteins and comes from a good supplier.

I count the days until our next hospital visit, the next verdict, the next high, or low. I'm not really living, I'm just in a holding pattern like one of the planes waiting to land at Heathrow, round and round until the next scan.

The days have ground by and at last we're back at the maternity wing. I'm now ten weeks pregnant. The nurse meets us at the door and tells us that Mr. Wright will see us after we have had the scan. We feel almost like one of the normal couples waiting for their scans, although most of them are at least sixteen weeks gone and have small telltale bulges under their sweaters. I can't wait for my bulge to start showing. I'm sure I'm walking about with my tummy stuck forward, so that any small bulge that appears is immediately noticeable.

This time we are in for a normal scan and so once again I sit and sip away at the jug of water that has been handed to me upon arrival. Still, this is different. Last time there was the fear and the apprehension because we knew something was wrong. I had been bleeding and was in a lot of pain. Now, at least as far as we know, there is nothing wrong. I've never felt so tense in all my life. These scans are like islands of rest in an ocean with waves so high they knock you sideways with a puff.

We're called in, my legs feel as wobbly as the jelly they put on my stomach. It's cold and sticky. Thank goodness Fiona is doing the scan. She is involved with the group and a good friend of Tina. It all helps. She's also good, very good. Before we have even had a chance to get in a panic she points out a tiny pulsating blob on the screen. Boom, boom, not more than a flicker, and yet strong as an ox. My heart just swells and swells with pride. Look, that's our little person in there, pumping away with its strong little heartbeat. Boom, boom, boom. You can't hear it, but you can see it. What a miracle, what a wonderful, extraordinary miracle. And it's our miracle.

A slow happy trickle of tears flows down my cheeks, tears of joy, fear, and also sadness for what was lost. Hope for the future, relief, pride, every emotion focussed on this flickering little heart on the screen. I can't actually believe it's inside me. Once the scanner is switched off it will feel like we have left the image of our pregnancy behind inside the machine. I know I'll start worrying again in a day or two, but right now I'm on top of the world. Peter just squeezes and squeezes my hand. We don't ever want to stop looking at the monitor.

As long as we can see it, it's real, and we know it's there. However, the waiting room is full of other couples, and finally Fiona has to switch off the monitor. She prints off a copy of the scan picture, the second for our collection, and we head back to see Mr. Wright.

Walking through the corridors, scan picture clenched tightly against my chest, I feel as if I'm going up to see the headmaster with my examination results. Mr. Wright looks at the scan picture and again helps us to make sense of the fuzzes and the blobs. He feels the pregnancy is well established in the womb, located in a good place, and that as far as he is concerned this is going to be a winner. He looks me straight in the eye as he says: "This is going to be fine. There is nothing to worry about. In fact, I really don't think I want to see you for at least the next five months."

He means it, and I trust him ... ish. We agree to book a scan at sixteen weeks, more for my peace of mind than anything else, but it will be routine, and we won't go back to Mr. Wright until the last weeks of the pregnancy. I walk out of the maternity wing on clouds. Outside is a little bench with tubs of daffodils each side. Peter parks me on the bench as he goes to fetch the car. A deep feeling of joy and contentment descends on me. If I were Badger or Bundy I would start purring. I look up at the sky and give thanks for the new life I now know I'm safely carrying.

As soon as we're home I call pappa and mamma. I've been rehearsing this in my mind for the past two weeks. "Mamma, I'm pregnant, it's in the right place, and we've seen the heart beat." It's saying those words that really brings the truth of it home to me, and we both burst out crying on the phone. Once we've recovered ourselves she tells me she had realised something was up, but this is further down the line and much better news than she had dared hope.

Later that evening, as we sit in the conservatory looking out onto our garden, we imagine a little person crawling about there on a blanket next Spring. Just think, this time it might really happen. Tiny glimmers of hope and light seep unseen through the cracks in our walls of defence. We're still not talking names, we're still not talking nurseries, but what we saw today was the absolute proof of a new chance.

"Well, isn't that just typical. As soon as you stop wanting it so badly it comes along." It's a comment I am hearing a lot lately. And then they go on to tell you about all the other people they know who miraculously fell pregnant the moment they filled in adoption papers or booked a roundtrip ticket to the other side of the world. As if we are the instigators of our own misfortune. Are they right? Well, even if they are, and I'm not so sure, you can't make yourself stop thinking about it, dreaming about it, longing for it. Just as you can't stop breathing, or going to sleep and waking up.

Children that ask don't get, or something like that. It's true that I had come to a stage where it really wasn't the be all and end all of my existence anymore, moving on, letting other areas of my life grow and develop. Accepting that Life has her own agenda. And of course the irony isn't lost on us, becoming pregnant when we least expect it. But to imply that someone becomes pregnant just because they turned a corner suggests that women suffering from miscarriages and infertility should just stop thinking about it so much and get on with their lives. A suggestion that is as hurtful as it is pointless. It just increases the sense of failure and stupidity that women already feel about not being able to produce a baby, and implies that you are really to blame for your own misfortunes!

Twelve weeks. Passing from the first to the second trimester. Not feeling so nauseous anymore. Loved feeling nauseous anyway. The more nauseous the better, at least it's a sign all is well. I'm tired and fazed out, but much less scared and worried than I thought I might be.

Mr. Wright's words still ring in my ears and I continue to trust him. What I would love though is to have a little window into my tummy to see what is going on. Just to be able to check in with the little whatsit and see if it's alright.

Peter is being rock solid and treats me like I'm a china doll. He still won't talk much about it, but this is his way of showing how much he cares. He has even started calling me pregno again, as well as referring to our little miracle as Junior, but that's as far as he will go on the name front. Four more weeks and we will have our next scan.

I can't resist telling him just before we have our third scan that I think it's a girl and that I want to call her Chiara if it is. Peter thinks this is complete nonsense and says: "If you're so sure, you'll let me name it if he turns out to be a boy?"

"Of course," I say, blissfully handing over this major area of responsibility to Peter, "since I know it will be a girl."

Five minutes later I'm eating my words. The scan picture is clearer than ever. We now see a head, a body, and little arms and legs that move! Still that proud little heart is thumping away. Then the radiographer asks if we want to know the baby's sex. Recalling our conversation in the waiting room only a few minutes ago we laugh

"Why not?"

"Well, don't rush out and buy everything in blue yet," she says, "but, it looks as if it could well be a little boy."

In the chair beside me a transformation takes place. Peter stirs, straightens his back, grasps my hand in an even firmer grasp, and stares at the monitor. I see it too now, and together we point out the wobbly bits to Peter.

"A boy," I hear him whisper, "a boy" ... and for the first time I catch a glimpse of the proud father that Peter is to become. The proud father of a son. Our relief and happiness know no bounds. Not because 'it' is a boy, but because by knowing 'it' is a boy 'it' has suddenly gained a far greater reality. We are expecting a son.

Back on the bench outside the maternity wing I dare to imagine that I'll be back here in November to deliver my baby. Next door is the main hospital building. I stare up at the floor where I spent those harrowing hours coming to terms with and losing my first two pregnancies. I haven't forgotten them, they are still with me now.

10th November, 1993

"Could I talk to Peter, it's Lysanne."

"Oh my God, you're not in labour are you?" It seems as if the whole office is waiting with bated breath for Junior to show himself.

"No, I'm not due for another two weeks, I just need to let him know something."

I laugh, I enjoy the attention and feel special.

"Actually darling," as Peter comes to the phone, "I just wanted to pop round to the maternity wing tonight to check if my waters aren't leaking."

"What do you mean, do you think you are going to have the baby now?"

"No, calm down, I just feel a little different today, and I'm losing some fluid. Maybe I've just become really incontinent."

"I'll come over right now," and in my mind I see Peter pulling on his coat and grabbing around for the car keys.

"Look, you're only five minutes from home, I'll call you if anything happens, but otherwise just come home at about five and we'll pop into maternity."

Quarter to five he is parked outside the house. I have my overnight bag standing ready in the hallway. I don't really think I'll need it, or maybe I do. I've been feeling different the last 24 hours.

Last weekend we finally bought some bits and pieces for 'Junior's' room, and I feel completely ready for him to come. I think I have a hunch, and yet it's no more than that. The only real thing that is happening is that I think I'm drip dripping water from the sac, but like I said to Peter, I could just be really incontinent.

It's been very quiet in my tummy for the past twelve hours, and I've slept like a log the past two nights. Anyway, rather than sit and speculate I decide the wisest thing is to just pop round to the maternity wing. They've been really wonderful, they know my history and they said I could always pop in if I was feeling at all concerned.

Peter drops me at the door and goes to park the car. I wait, sitting on the same bench where I had sat five months ago. In the twilight I feel I'm saying goodbye to one part of my life and hello to another.

Fanciful thinking, I tell myself, *nothing is happening, you've two weeks left to go.*

We go in together, but I take charge. I feel so confident and so calm. The nurse shows me to one of the labour rooms and asks me to wait on the bed for the midwife. She reassures me there is no problem about me popping in. Peter and I stare at each other as we hear a scream from down the corridor, then we burst out laughing, we've still got it to come.

The midwife hears what I have to say and checks the cervix. She also takes a sample to see if there is any amniotic fluid escaping to places where it shouldn't. A dull ache has started in my lower back, rather like the early warning pain that heralds a period.

The woman down the end of the corridor continues giving birth loudly. I tell Peter to put a sock in my mouth if I make such a noise. The nurse pops in again with a cup of tea, and I ask her to check if the room with the birthing pool has been booked for tonight. I've wanted to give birth in the water for as long as I can remember, and we are lucky that our maternity hospital has many years of experience conducting water births. She checks, the pool is free. *This is the night,* I think to myself.

The midwife returns with the results. The results are negative, the sac is not leaking. She tells me to get dressed and to go home, now getting a little short with me as the screams from down the corridor become even louder and more frequent. "And yet I feel something is happening," I say to Peter as I heave myself across the bed. And in that instant I feel my waters break. Peter is aghast and despite having read all the books stands pointing to the pool of water and asks if I have just wet myself.

"In a manner of speaking," I say. "Now go and get the midwife again." She walks in five minutes later with a terribly annoyed look on her face. I'm becoming nuisance of the night. But then she sees the drenched sheets and admits grudgingly that my waters must have broken. "You're not in labour yet, and it can be tomorrow morning before you even start having contractions. We'll pop you up into the labour ward and they will keep an eye on you there."

In the meantime I'm starting to feel the most curious sensations in my lower body, and not at all pleasant. As they help me into the wheelchair to take me upstairs I almost pass out. Not in labour, what's this then?

10th November, 20.00hrs

I have my own room in the labour ward and the ward sister is rushing about showing Peter how the TV works. Never mind, we already missed East Enders. There is supposed to be a phone and she rushes off to find it. I'm sure I'm having contractions, and I couldn't care less about the phone right now, but everyone seems to assume I won't be in labour for hours yet. If this isn't labour, what will it be like?

I want to have a water birth without any pain relief. I've been saying that I want to do this the natural way. I've been in enough pain with the miscarriages to know I can handle a lot, especially if there is a baby at the end of it. That was the theory at least, until a few hours ago, but if this isn't the start of labour, I'm in for a big surprise. The ward sister goes off duty and is replaced by a less facilities-oriented colleague. She immediately agrees to put me on a monitor and after a while says that there are some niggly contractions there, but by no means the full works. She tells me to go and have a warm bath down the corridor. Peter helps me off the bed.

We shuffle down the corridor and look into the wards where the brand new mums are lying with their babies. Somehow Peter manages to hoist me into the bath, and then the real work begins.

Contractions are great, I'd rather have those than period pain. They come and then they go away again, leaving you with a nice long breather in between. After half an hour we think they're getting stronger and more regular. Peter goes off in search of the nurse and I keep repeating to myself: "If I can handle this contraction, I can handle the next."

Peter comes back with the ward sister and the midwife from downstairs. I smile at her apologetically. "I'm sorry, I'm not being a very good girl here am I?" But she laughs and tells me I'm doing great. They manage to get me back on the bed and decide to check how far, if at all, I'm dilated.

Five centimetres.

We've been in there less than four hours and I'm five centimetres dilated. With a grin on her face the midwife tells me she is going to take me back down to the labour rooms where they have started running the labour bath for me.

I'm so curious to see what the little person is going to look like. I'm in a daze and yet completely focussed. The daze blocks out all irrelevant information like clocks and modesty, and I'm totally concentrated on helping my body do what it knows best. I've had years of period pain to prepare me for this, and a couple of miscarriages where the pain resulted in absolutely zilch. Now we will have our little boy at the end of this, and with every contraction he is coming closer. As I'm wheeled into the labour room adjacent to the pool a beautiful big Nigerian midwife asks me what kind of pain relief I want.

"Nothing," I almost shout, "I just want to be in that pool."

"Good, good," she says, a big grin on her face.

The other midwife, water births requiring at least two midwives to be present, is from New Zealand, and tiny. I need to be seven centimetres dilated to be allowed in the pool, and the half hour on the bed waiting to get there is painful.

Finally I'm allowed to waddle into the room where the pool is. As soon as I sink into the lukewarm water all the niggly in-between pains disappear, and all I have to deal with are the real contractions. The Nigerian midwife asks Peter whether he's getting into the pool with me. This has been a sore point ever since I decided on a water birth. Peter has been adamant, he doesn't want to be in the pool with me. However, put on the spot, he now turns around to me and says: "Well, what do you want me to do?"

"GET IN!!"

In a second he has stripped down to his boxer shorts and comes to sit behind me, legs either side of my body. I lean back against him, and for a moment there is complete peace. Our two midwives sit at either end of the pool. Someone is humming a lullaby. We really are the United Nations in there, and our little boy will be the only Englishman in the room. After every second contraction they check his heartbeat. Very quickly I'm fully dilated and they tell me to start pushing. Having been calm and going with the flow the whole way, I now suddenly seem to lose it.

Birth

Birth, birthing, giving birth,
Mother Earth.
The pain, the joyful pain,
wave after wave, a tormenting refrain.

The waiting over, to see you at last.
Gift of the Gods, of ages past.
Ugly bundle, into life you are thrust,
so helpless, so wanted
accepted in trust.

Now we're together, the battle is won.
Your mother loves you,
my child, my son.

11th November 1993, 02.30 am

"He's coming out the wrong way."

"No he's not, he's just touching on your rectal nerves. Don't push now, now push, breathe, good girl, breathe, big push, one more big push...... Wow, the little guy has got his elbow sticking out sideways."

"Oh well, who needs their perineum anyway?" I moan.

"We'll sew you up again."

And then suddenly, as quickly as this last phase of the birthing process had started, it's all over. With a not so elegant twist of his body, young Karl comes blinking into this world and greets us with a short sharp cry.

I feel Peter's hot tears in my neck, and my own are tumbling down my cheeks and dripping into the water. Then he is laid on my tummy and we stare each other deep in the eyes for the first time. He looks recycled, his eyes look like he's been here before. He already looks wise. We know each other the instant we see each other and our bond starts to form. From here on, for better or worse, our lives are forever intertwined.

I sit in the warm water holding my child, my man sits behind me and holds us both. The moment I had almost stopped daring to dream of is finally here. I kiss Karl on the tip of his nose. and lean my head back against Peter's shoulder.

"Welcome home little man, I've carried you for two and a half years."

A gift

Through a gathering of clouds
a shaft of light
falls;
warming our hearts,
rekindling our spirits,
and bringing great joy.

KARL WILLEM HELGE GULLÖ

A true gift indeed !

For further information and support you might like to contact:

The Ectopic Pregnancy Trust
The Hillingdon Hospital
Pield Heath Road
Uxbridge, Middlesex UB8 3NN
Tel: 01895 238025
www.ectopic.org.uk

The Miscarriage Association,
Wakefield,
West Yorkshire.
Telephone 01924 200799.
Scottish Office Helpline
Tel: 0131 334 8883
www.miscarriage.association.care4free.net

British Association for Counselling
1 Regent Place
Rugby
Warwickshire CV21 2PJ
Tel: 01788 550 899
www.bac.co.uk

Stillbirth and Neonatal Death Society
(SANDS)
28 Portland Place
London
W1N 4DE
020 7436 5881
support@uk-sands.org

British Association for Adoption and
Fostering
Skyline House
200 Union Street
London SE1 OLY
Tel: 020 7593 2000
www.baaf.org.uk

Child Death Helpline
Tel: 020 7829 8685

Cruse – Bereavement Care
Cruse House
126 Sheen Road
Richmond
Surrey TW9 1UR
Tel: 020 8940 4818

National Association for the Childless
20 Folgate
London E1 6DB
Tel: 020 7247 1080

Care
Stair House Farm
Stair
Mauchline
Ayrshire
KA5 5HW
Tel: 01292 591741

Child
Charter House
43 St Leonards Road
Bexhill on Sea
East Sussex
TN40 1JA
Tel: 01424 732361 24 hour answering

COTS
Loandhu Cottage
Gruids
Lairg
Sutherland, Scotland
IV27 4ES
Tel: 01549 402401

Foresight (Association for the Promotion
of Pre-conceptual Care)
28 The Paddock
Godalming
Surrey
GU7 1XD
Tel: 01483 427839

Action on Pre-eclampsia
31-33 College Road,
Harrow, Middlesex, HA1 1EJ
Helpline: 020 84274217

The Child Bereavement Trust
Aston House
West Wycombe
High Wycombe
Buckinghamshire
HP14 2AG
Tel: 01494 446648

Cover Design: The Digital Canvas Company
                  Forres
                  Scotland
                  bookcovers@digican.co.uk

Layout: Stephen M.L. Young
                  LaTouveilhe@mac.com

Font: Adobe Garamond (11pt)

Copies of this book can be ordered via the Internet:

                  www.librario.com

or from:

                  Librario Publishing Ltd
                  Brough House
                  Milton Brodie
                  Kinloss
                  Moray IV36 2UA
                  Tel /Fax No 01343 850 617